Generati

First Edition Design Publishing

Generation Why?

ISBN 978-1622-875-77-1 PRINT
ISBN 978-1622-875-76-4 EBOOK

LCCN 2014936889

April 2014

Published and Distributed by
First Edition Design Publishing, Inc.
P.O. Box 20217, Sarasota, FL 34276-3217
www.firsteditiondesignpublishing.com

Generation Why?

?

Dan Greenup

Table of Contents

Preface

I don't like being lied to. Who does? In school, I was told I was a highly-evolved accident whose distant ancestor was pond chemicals. According to my teachers, God didn't make me. I came from pond scum. Apparently, all of my thoughts and feelings were just the result of chemical reactions in the brain. I had no mind of my own, because I didn't have a mind at all. I wasn't free, because everything I did was predetermined by the makeup of my brain. I was told the only purpose in life was to pass my genes on to the next generation. In other words, I was an accident in a world filled with death, pain and suffering, and my only purpose was to bring another accident into this world. Depressing? Welcome to high school biology.

These days, people are shocked when young people commit suicide. You'll hear them say "They just had so much to live for!" Really? Like what? If evolution is true, life's a cruel accident. What's the point of living? Is it about getting filthy rich? Well, being the richest person in the cemetery won't do a lot of good. Is it about partying and having a good time? How boring! Besides, what's the point of being the happiest-looking corpse in the morgue? Is it about leaving a legacy? Who cares? I'd be dead, so I wouldn't be able to enjoy everyone loving on my memory.

Indeed, when you tell young people they are mindless animals who can't control themselves, why would anyone be surprised when they murder their classmates? If there is no God, what's right and wrong is a matter of personal opinion. Anything goes. Why would I obey laws? They're nothing more than one group's opinions about right and wrong. Who cares what they think? Why would their atoms be more "moral" than mine? So, if murdering my classmates is good for me, why not do it? After all, what's true for you isn't true for me, right?

Ultimately, this is why people like evolution. We're supposedly the most 'evolved' things around, so we get to be in charge. Everyone likes to play God. What if kids are depressed about being told they are completely worthless? Survival of the fittest, they'll say. How charming.

Fortunately, evolution is a lie. The Bible says God created everything, and it's so obvious that people are "without excuse."[1] Put differently, the Bible says there's no excuse for atheism. The question isn't whether or not God exists. No, the question is how you feel about God. Do you love Him, or do you hate Him? There's no middle ground.

Of course, this is the God of the Bible we're talking about. We're not talking about all of the made-up versions of "God" out there. Sure, it's more comfortable to believe in a "God" of our own making, but that's no different than worshiping a wooden statue. You can take your 'coexist' bumper sticker and throw it in the trash, because it should say 'contradict.' All religions can't be true. There is only one way to God, and Jesus said "I am the way."[2] Everything else is a detour people stumble onto trying to avoid the Way, and I have firsthand experience.

I spent the first 21 years of my life running from God. Now, I never fully bought into evolution. The idea that everything created itself seemed ridiculous. How does something that doesn't exist make itself? It made no sense. "Chance did it," my biology teacher would say, but blind luck seemed like a stretch. Try telling your biology teacher chance ate your homework. How unlucky!

In all seriousness, if you saw a snowman, would you think it evolved from snowflakes by chance over millions of years? If you saw a sandcastle, would you say that it evolved from grains of sand by chance? If you said yes, your family would stage an intervention. Still, my teachers seemed pretty enthusiastic about evolution. They were the 'experts,' so, I figured God could've used evolution. Eventually, this also seemed ridiculous. It contradicts the first page of the Bible! I mean, if you can't trust page one, how can you trust the rest of it?

For my part, I didn't care about the details. I was too busy living the good life. I thought I had it all. Certainly, I was what society would consider a 'good' kid. I didn't do drugs. I didn't sleep around. I got good grades. Gold stars all around! Truth be told, I was an egomaniac. What, you couldn't tell?

For some reason, I thought that unless you were Hitler, you were going to Heaven. You just have to be good enough, and I definitely thought I qualified. What about the bad stuff I had done? No big deal. All of the good stuff would cancel it out. Well, there's no point system to get into Heaven. You're either perfect, or you're not getting in.[3] I thought I was pretty awesome, but even I could see perfection wasn't going to happen. I thought the "Big Guy" and I were cool, but I found out that to be cool with God, you have to be cool with Jesus.

No, it wasn't dramatic. I didn't have a major tragedy. I was selfish. I knew I couldn't live up to God's standard, and I didn't want to be punished for it. I asked Jesus to save me. How's that for self-preservation?

You've heard the saying "time heals all wounds." Nothing could be further from the truth. Time won't heal all wounds. Jesus will. By His wounds, we are healed.[4] That's what this book is all about. There is a real answer to the why question, and it's much better than anything you could ever make up.

The Why Question

For as long as anyone can remember, in one way or another, human beings have asked themselves the following question: why am I here? In recent years, the common answers to this age-old question have changed quite a bit. Most people, it seems, have simply given up on finding a concrete answer. After all, a great many individuals believe "there is no such thing as truth." Well, is that a true statement? If it is, then there's such a thing as truth. Similarly, a good number of people maintain what is true for one person isn't true for another. Yet, if two people jumped off of a bridge, the Law of Gravity is going to apply to both of them. Still, many individuals acknowledge that truth exists, but they say human beings can't be certain of it. Of course, how could they know that for sure, if we can't be certain anything is true? Other people claim all religions lead to God. This must be false, however, because all religions frequently contradict each other. For example, Christians believe Jesus is God, while Muslims deny Jesus is God. Jesus can't be God and not God at the same time, so Islam and Christianity cannot both be correct. Since all religions make exclusive claims, they can't all be true about God. Clearly, there is absolute spiritual truth, and only one of the many beliefs out there can truly explain why we're all here.

Now, a few people aren't sure if anyone is here at all. They say "everything is an illusion." But, if that's true, it wouldn't be a very good idea to take their word for it. Without a doubt, we're all really here, and the most popular explanation for where human beings came from is evolution. Evolution is the belief that everything made itself over billions of years and God had nothing to do with it. It is widely thought that billions of years ago, a tiny body of matter began expanding and this gave rise to our current universe, though no one is quite sure where this matter came from. The earth was eventually formed and as it cooled down, rain began to fall. Some time later, non-living chemicals floating around in this water somehow gave rise to a living, single-celled organism with extremely complex genetic information known as DNA. Through natural selection, this simple organism became more complex over millions of years, despite the fact natural selection actually leads to a decrease in genetic information. So, according to evolution, human beings are a highly unlikely accident that can trace their ancestry back to rearranged pond chemicals. While fashionable, evolution doesn't completely satisfy the 'why' question for many people. To fill in some details, particularly what happens to people when they die, many people have turned to religions such as Buddhism and New Ageism. Other individuals, trying to shed some more light on where everybody came from, believe that aliens originally put humans on the earth. Yet, there is an entirely different explanation for how everyone got here.

The Bible, which Christians believe is the written Word of God, records that "In the beginning God created the heaven and the earth."[1] God created a perfect world, where everything "was very good."[2] There was no suffering or death.[3] Unfortunately, this perfect world was ruined by the rebellion of the first man and the first woman, Adam and Eve. God told them not to eat the fruit of a certain tree, for if they did, they would "surely die."[4] Well, they ate from the tree anyway, and their disobedience brought suffering, death and separation from God into the world.[5] All humans have inherited Adam's sinful nature and naturally, all humans have broken God's law.[6] Since God is perfectly just, everyone is subject to eternal separation from His presence while being punished for their sins.[7] Fortunately, God has done something about it. The Bible says, "For God so loved the world, that he gave his only begotten Son, that whosoever believeth in him should not perish, but have everlasting life."[8] Jesus Christ, fully God and fully man,[9] took upon Himself the punishment for everyone's sin by dying on the Cross.[10] Three days later He rose again, showing His power over all things, including death.[11] Anyone who trusts in Jesus alone for the forgiveness of their sins will receive eternal life with God.[12] Overall, we are here to have a personal relationship with God.

So, where did everyone really come from? Well, there are two kinds of science. There's experimental science and historical science. Experimental science deals with the here and now. It involves doing experiments in the present and drawing conclusions. This type of science has led to many advances in medicine and technology. Historical science, on the other hand, deals with the past. It uses observations from the present to explain the past. After all, scientists can't experiment directly on past events and history can't repeat itself. Since these experiments are so limited, a person's beliefs on what happened in the past play a big role in interpreting the evidence. A person that believes in the record of the Bible will reach different conclusions from people that don't believe the Bible. Evolution and the biblical account of creation are both examples of historical science, and a person's belief in one or the other will greatly shape their answer to the 'why' question. When picking one or the other, and choosing from one of the many answers to the 'why' question out there, everyone must keep in mind the following questions: how do I know, and what if I'm wrong?

Living in a Material World

Evolution

I hate to break it to you, but you've been lied to. Shocking, right? From elementary school on, we were all told that the universe created itself by chance, non-living chemicals formed into a living organism with complex genetic information and that through natural selection, this organism grew more complex over millions of years. What's wrong with this account of history? Well, none of these unproven assumptions are supported by scientific observation. Remember that experimental science, which has given the world modern medicine, men on the moon and other remarkable achievements, is different from historical science. Historical science attempts to piece together what happened in the past. Of course, the past can't be repeated and experimental science still hasn't given us the time machine. As a result, any explanation about the past requires a bunch of assumptions. Evolutionist scientist Stephen Jay Gould put it best when he said that "Our ways of learning about the world are strongly influenced by the social preconceptions and biased modes of thinking that each scientist must apply to any problem."[1] In other words, everyone has biases, so our assumptions about the past are going to be different depending on what we believe about why we're here. Christians believe in God, and the biblical account of creation, while evolutionists deny that God exists. They believe the material world, or nature, is all that there is. So, which theory of history is accurate? The account that is better supported by observations from the experimental sciences is correct. In light of scientific observation, evolution doesn't hold up too well.

The 'Big Bang'

According to evolution, the universe created itself billions of years ago. Yet, in order for it to create itself, it would have already had to exist. How does something that doesn't exist create itself? The jury is still out. Regardless, the story goes that in the beginning, all matter and energy was in a tiny dot called a 'point of singularity.' All of a sudden, this dot rapidly inflated itself like a balloon and expanded to roughly the present size of the universe. Naturally, this begs the question, where'd the matter come from? It couldn't have come from nothing because nothing, the absence of something, comes from nothing. This is not only common sense, but also a fundamental scientific law. The First Law of Thermodynamics, also known as the Law of Conservation of Energy, states that energy can't be created or destroyed. It can only be converted from one form to another. Since matter is a form of energy, matter also cannot be created or destroyed. So, according to evolutionists, the matter that inflated itself during the 'Big Bang' appeared out of nowhere in spite of scientific law. While this is hard to believe, evolutionists also don't know what caused the dot of matter and energy to inflate itself.

After all, the Law of Inertia states that objects in motion will continue in motion while objects at rest will stay at rest, unless an outside force acts upon them. A good example of this would be a golf ball. It rests on the ground until it is hit with a club. Once hit, it flies through the air, until gravity and friction bring it back to a resting position on the ground. How, then, could a tiny dot of matter move itself in spite of scientific law? It's safe to say that scientists haven't worked that part out yet. On the other hand, some frustrated evolutionists assume the universe must've have always existed. Claiming that the universe didn't have a beginning, however, creates more problems than it solves.

For starters, we know from the First Law of Thermodynamics that matter and energy can't be created or destroyed. Well, the Second Law of Thermodynamics states that the amount of usable energy in the universe is decreasing. The effects of this law are all around us. Clothing fades, buildings decay and our bodies break down. Eventually, since new energy can't be created, there will be no usable energy left in the universe. Life as we know it will cease to exist. That bit of cheerful news aside, if the universe had always existed, there would already be no usable energy left and none of us would be here. As if that weren't enough, the Second Law of Thermodynamics presents another problem for evolutionists, whether they believe in a 'Big Bang' or an eternal universe. Since the universe is losing usable energy, and it can't be replaced, where did all of the usable energy come from in the first place?

It's at this point, usually, where evolutionists try turning the tables. They ask, "If God created the universe, who created God then?" While this seems like a profound question, it's really a lot like asking what the color blue tastes like. Everything that has a beginning has a cause. For example, the Space Needle hasn't always existed, and it didn't just pop out of nowhere for no reason. It was the result of careful planning and many months of hard work. Well, the Bible clearly states that God is eternal.[2] He has always been and He always will be. Since God is the Creator of the whole universe, including time, He doesn't have a beginning in time. He is not subject to time because He created it. So, because God didn't have a beginning, He doesn't have a cause. On the other hand, the First and Second Laws of Thermodynamics show that the universe had a beginning. Since everything which has a beginning has a cause, the universe must've had a cause. So, what caused matter to create itself from nothing? What was the driving force behind this matter being squeezed into a tiny dot, and what caused it to begin expanding? For many evolutionists, chance is what brought everything into being.

If, by chance, this explanation sounds a little flaky, it is probably because chance isn't actually a thing. Chance is a word that refers to mathematical probabilities, or odds. It can't cause events to happen. If I told a police officer that chance made me run that red light, the officer probably isn't going to let me off the hook. Another good example is a coin flip. If a coin is flipped, and heads comes up, chance didn't make the coin do anything. Real causes could range from whether the coin started heads up or tails up, how high the coin was flipped, how dense the atmosphere was or how many revolutions the coin made, to name a few possibilities. In other words, chance can't cause anything. Saying that chance caused the universe is like saying that nothing caused the universe, but ultimately, that is what the 'Big Bang' claims. Also known as cosmic evolution, the 'Big Bang' hasn't been observed and it can't be tested in a lab. This isn't a surprise for a theory of history, but being incompatible with scientific laws isn't exactly going to generate a lot of confidence in the theory. While many people will rightly label the 'Big Bang' unscientific, it might be better to say that it just requires a lot of faith. Of course, the faith required to believe in the 'Big Bang' isn't nearly as great as the leap of faith needed to accept chemical evolution.

The Origin of Life

It is thought that, after a tiny dot of energy and matter inflated itself and expanded, the earth was born. It is also believed that over time, the earth cooled and rain began to fall. Of course, this hasn't been observed and it can't be tested in a lab, so evolutionists accept that this happened by faith. What took place in this rainwater, however, truly demands a belief in miracles without a Miracle-Giver. Evolutionists believe in something called 'abiogenesis.' Also known as chemical evolution, 'abiogenesis' is the idea that non-living chemicals gave rise to a living single-celled organism with extremely complex genetic information known as DNA. If that seems more like science fiction than science, it is probably because according to scientific observation, 'abiogenesis' is actually impossible.

The scientific Law of Biogenesis states that life can only come from life. Living organisms, according to scientific law, can only come from other living organisms. The experiments of Louis Pasteur confirmed this law in the late 19th century, oddly around the same time evolution began growing in popularity. So, how did lifeless chemicals floating around in a pond create a living organism? Even people who believe in evolution aren't sure. Evolutionist professor Paul Davies admitted that

"Nobody knows how a mixture of lifeless chemicals spontaneously organized themselves into the first living cell."[3] As fellow evolutionist Gordy Slack said, "Evolution should be able to explain, in theory at least, all the way back to the very first organism that could replicate itself through biological or chemical processes. And to understand that organism fully, we would simply have to know what came before it. And right now we are nowhere close."[4] Curiously, this hasn't stopped either of these gentlemen from believing in evolution. Since they believe the material world is all that there is, and God doesn't exist, they must have blind faith that scientific law was once violated and that life came from non-life through chemical evolution. Yet, this is hardly the only 'miracle' that evolutionists are forced to accept.

For example, deoxyribonucleic acid, more commonly known as DNA, is an information storage system in all living organisms that encodes genetic instructions. DNA is so remarkable, that evolutionist and biologist Richard Dawkins noted "There is enough information capacity in a single human cell to store the *Encyclopaedia Britannica*, all 30 volumes of it, three or four times over."[5] So, where did this elaborate DNA code come from? After all, the *Encyclopaedia Britannica* didn't just write itself, so why would we assume that DNA wrote itself? On top of that, DNA requires a complex molecular machine known as a ribosome to decode it, but the instructions to build ribosomes are on the DNA. So which came first? Philosopher Sir Karl Popper once said this problem was "a really vicious circle, it seems, for any attempt to form a model or theory of the genesis of the genetic code."[6] Explaining where DNA came from is made even harder by the scientific Laws of Information.[7]

Stored on their DNA, living things contain enormous amounts of information. This encoded information is the blueprint for building and using the various parts of a living organism. The first scientific Law of Information tells us that something material can't create something non-material, like a thought. Well, the second scientific Law of Information states that information is a non-material entity. For example, let's say a person has two identical DVD's. One DVD is filled with information, and the other DVD is blank. If both discs are weighed, they will weigh the same. It wouldn't matter how much information is added or erased, the discs will continue to weigh the same. Why is this?

Information is non-material. It doesn't have mass, so it has no weight. Matter, on the other hand, has mass. It is weighable. All non-material entities, such as consciousness, thoughts and information, have no weight. This presents quite the problem for evolutionists, considering their belief that matter is all there is. How could matter and energy create something non-material like information? Obviously, if you poured a bunch of ink onto a piece of paper, a book isn't going to evolve by chance. So, why would we assume genetic information evolved from pond chemicals? With this in mind, it's clear that chemical evolution has more in common with a children's fable than a legitimate theory of history. The fanciful story-telling of evolutionists doesn't stop with the origin of life though, for believing that natural selection turned a single-celled organism into every living creature on the planet requires an active imagination in its own right.

Survival of the Fittest

If you've attended a public high school, you've probably heard about those pesky DDT-resistant mosquitoes. It goes a little something like this: "Mosquitoes have evolved a resistance to DDT and…" Altogether now, class… "that's evolution in action!" Sure, evolutionists don't know where the universe or life came from, but that's neither here nor there. Those mosquitoes, they'll say, are proof that pond chemicals are our distant ancestor. If that seems like a bit of a stretch, upon further review, it's actually just a lie. Natural selection, affectionately known by the catchphrase 'survival of the fittest,' is a process where existing genetic information from an organism is selected so that organism is more likely to survive in a certain environment. No new genes are created. In fact, natural selection gets rid of genetic information, because certain genes are chosen and other genes are bred out. Over time, genes that aren't selected for an environment are eliminated and there is less information in a population. The DDT-resistant mosquitoes are a good example.

A DDT-resistant mosquito is more adapted to an environment with DDT, but those mosquitoes that haven't adapted die. The mosquitoes that die don't pass on their genes, so there is less genetic information in the mosquito population overall. Well, there would need to be a massive increase in genetic information for a one-celled organism to turn into you or me over millions of years. After all, a single-celled organism doesn't have the information to build arms, legs, eyes, noses or a brain, among other things. Since natural selection always chooses from existing information, and never creates information, where did genetic information come from? Also, since natural selection causes a loss of genetic information, how could a single-celled organism become more complex?

If these questions were asked in class, teachers would probably become uncomfortable. In response, they would likely return to those DDT-resistant mosquitoes. They might ask "If DDT-resistant mosquitoes aren't examples of evolution in action, then what is?" The answer is simple. Natural selection isn't evolution. In reality, it hurts the case for evolution. Natural selection is variation within a kind. It is also known as adaptation or speciation. For example, a wolf, a dingo and a poodle are different types of dogs, but they are still dogs. Those DDT-resistant mosquitoes are still mosquitoes. They haven't turned into anything else. Evolutionists believe that one kind of animal, like a dog, came from another kind of animal, like a rat. That sort of thing has never been observed, and natural selection sheds some light on why this doesn't happen. The selection process doesn't create genetic information. In fact, natural selection reduces genetic information over time. Recall that evolution is the belief that the universe created itself by chance over billions of years. Nothing somehow made matter, non-living chemicals somehow made a living organism with DNA and obviously, this organism somehow became more complex in spite of natural selection, not because of it. Evolution is not natural selection. On the contrary, natural selection is another scientific observation that makes evolution appear all the more fantastical.

Realizing that natural selection is no friend of evolution, most evolutionists have looked elsewhere to find a way for genetic information to be added to an organism. These days, evolutionists have settled on genetic mutations. Mutations are copying mistakes in DNA code. Down syndrome, hemophilia and cystic fibrosis are a few of the more well-known disorders that are a result of genetic mutations. Again, mutations tell us nothing about where DNA came from in the first place, but they also don't lead to an increase of genetic information. For starters, mutations corrupt genetic information. They scramble the letters of DNA code in any number of ways. Mutations create new traits by corrupting existing genetic information, but they don't create new information. Now, these new traits aren't always a bad thing, as evolutionists are quick to point out. A common example is the existence of wingless beetles on a windy island. For a beetle living on a windy island, wings wouldn't be fun, because flying would put them at a higher risk for being swept off to sea. A mutation that produced the loss of wings would be helpful. Here's the catch: the beetle's loss of wings is a loss of genetic information. It might be a beneficial trait, but it is still a loss of information. So, with this in mind, how could a one-celled organism turn into a human over millions of years?

Surely, sex had to come into play at some point, but where did sex come from? Obviously, humans have sex, and single-celled organisms don't. An asexual organism would've had to develop sexual reproductive organs, but how could that have happened? Sexual reproduction can only take place when both genders have the complementary parts at the same time. If one gender evolved first, it would've died without a mate. Males couldn't have evolved first, because they wouldn't have been able to reproduce without females. Likewise, females couldn't have evolved first, because they wouldn't have been able to reproduce without males. For sexual reproduction to work, you need males and females with the proper boy parts and girl parts. Which gender came first, and how could it have survived without a mate? Clearly, evolutionists still haven't found a mechanism that links a one-celled organism to a human, but as we have seen, this is not the only case of a 'missing link' in evolutionary theory.

Atheism

Since evolution is a theory of history that attempts to explain creation without a Creator, evolution is atheism's account for how everyone got here. Simply put, atheism is the belief that there is no God.[8] The belief that God doesn't exist, of course, requires faith. Now, there are many flavors of atheism. One of the most popular is agnosticism. Generally, an agnostic believes humans can't know God. Of course, if no knowledge of God is possible, how is it that the agnostic knows this? Often, agnostics will respond that "something can only be true if it is proved scientifically." Well, can that statement be proved 'scientifically'? It certainly can't, so the statement is false by its own standard. Regardless, agnosticism is a common belief. While popular, there are several other branches of atheism, most of which are attempts to find something meaningful in a world that is thought to have no plan, no purpose and no hope. After all, evolution, the atheist account of how everyone got here, claims that human beings are unlikely accidents whose only purpose in life is passing their genes on to the next generation. This gloomy outlook is based on the assumption that the material world, or nature, is all that there is. It is this belief in materialism that is at the heart of evolution and, naturally, all forms of atheism.

Materialism

When people think of materialism, shopping malls and infomercials might be the first things that pop in their head. While materialism usually refers to consumerism, it is also the name of a philosophical system. Materialism is the belief that the universe is only made up of matter. Also called naturalism, materialists believe nature is all that there is. This assumption, however, isn't consistent with the world around us. First off, if the universe is only made of material things, our thoughts are nothing more than chemical reactions in the brain. C.S Lewis pointed out that if this were true, "then all our present thoughts are mere accidents—the accidental by-product of the movement of atoms. And this holds for the thoughts of the materialists and astronomers as well as for anyone else's." Lewis reasoned that "if their thoughts—i.e. of materialism and astronomy—are merely accidental by-products, why should we believe them to be true?"[9] In other words, if materialism were true, there would be no logical reason to believe that anything is true, including the idea of materialism itself. On top of that, if our thoughts are determined by the makeup of our brain, there's no such thing as being a 'free-thinker.'

Indeed, if our thoughts are just a result of chemical reactions, we can't help what we believe. For example, when someone believes that God doesn't exist, it is only because this belief has been predetermined by the makeup of their brain. They have no mind of their own. Atheists often say that "religion is a crutch for the weak-minded," but considering that atheists don't really believe the mind exists, this statement doesn't make a whole lot of sense. In fact, if all of our beliefs are the result of chemical reactions, why would the 'thoughts' of one person be trusted over another person's 'thoughts?' Since they both obey the same laws of chemistry, whose atoms do we trust? As evolutionist and atheist J.B.S. Haldane noted, "If my mental processes are determined wholly by the motions of atoms in my brain, I have no reason to suppose my beliefs are true. They may be sound chemically, but that does not make them sound logically."[10]

With this in mind, if the material world is all that there is, why does logic exist at all? If I went running, I'm not going to be worried about tripping over some logic. This is because logic, like reason, consciousness, thoughts and information, are all non-material. They aren't physical entities. So, the consistent atheist can't believe logic, reason, consciousness, thoughts and information exist. Atheist William B. Provine once stated that evolution, atheism's account of where everybody came from, clearly leads a person to conclude "There are no gods, no purposes, no goal-directed forces of any kind." He went on to say "There is no life after death. When I die, I am absolutely certain that I am going to be dead. That's the end for me. There is no ultimate foundation for ethics, no ultimate meaning to life, and no free will for humans, either."[11] There you have it. According to evolution and atheism, you and I are nothing more than mindless, soulless robots. Why are we here? It's simple, really. We're here to pass on our genes to the next generation. That's all. There is no greater purpose, no freedom, and no hope. As if that weren't enough, there's also no difference between right and wrong.

The Moral of the Story

People really don't like being told what they can and can't do. This has led a great many people to become atheists. If there is no God, after all, there are no moral absolutes. There is no such thing as right and wrong. People aren't 'free,' of course, because all of their 'thoughts' are just the result of chemical reactions. Still, people like to 'think' that they can "do as they please," in spite of the makeup of their brain. At first, not having any rules sounds like a lot of fun, but this presents many problems. If what is right is decided by human opinion, then anything goes. If I think it is right to steal your cell phone, for example, there's nothing stopping me from taking it. Naturally, you wouldn't like it. You would call it unfair and wrong, but on what grounds? Why is your opinion greater than my opinion? Better yet, why are the chemical reactions in your brain more moral than mine? If what is right is set by human opinion, nothing I do to you is wrong. So, clearly, people that don't believe in God can't really say anything is definitively right or wrong.

Atheists are quick to respond that "most people know the difference between right and wrong." They think the majority should decide what's right and wrong. Initially, this sounds quite appealing. It has a democratic feel to it. Unfortunately, this didn't work out so well in the 20th century, particularly in Nazi Germany. Millions of people were murdered in the name of creating a 'master race.' Most people would rightly find Hitler's attempt to speed up the 'evolutionary process' horrible and obviously immoral, but the majority of Germans at the time thought it was right. If a person doesn't believe in God, and His absolute moral code, that person can't say what happened in Nazi Germany was definitively wrong. In fact, atheists often say that since "there are no moral absolutes, we should be tolerant of other people's morals." Well, why 'should' we? By saying we 'should' be tolerant, the atheist is saying toleration is a moral absolute. That's not very tolerant. Regardless, many atheists over the years have decided to condemn Hitler, but by what standard? Why should their preferences have any more authority over the preferences of anyone else?

Now, this is not to say that atheists are bad people. Without a doubt, atheists can be moral people, according to another belief system's definition of course. Yet, by behaving morally, they are being inconsistent with their worldview. They must borrow a moral code from a different belief system, since atheism doesn't supply one. Whether an atheist is a murderer or a detective, according to their beliefs, there is no difference between murdering someone and putting a murderer behind bars. In other words, atheists have no objective basis for their behavior, good or bad. It is all just a matter of personal preference. On the contrary, when a Christian commits a moral crime, such as lying, that person is being inconsistent with their beliefs because they have been commanded not to lie.[12] When Christians act with compassion, they are behaving consistently with their beliefs, because Christians have been commanded to love even their enemies.[13] If there is no God, there is no ultimate authority on what a person can and can't do. This begs the question, why have laws at all?

If what is right and wrong varies from person to person, it would seem odd to punish someone for a 'crime.' What one person considers a crime, another person might find perfectly acceptable behavior. On top of that, as we've discussed, atheism also teaches that humans don't have free will. Well, if human actions are all the result of chemical reactions in the brain, how can a person be held responsible for their behavior? Law enforcement would cease to exist, for if people can't help what they do, how can they be prosecuted for wrongdoing? We don't take cars to court when they break down, so why blame someone for the makeup of their brain? Perhaps this is why many atheists say "people shouldn't judge." This is, however, a very judgmental statement. Why are they judging other people for judging? They obviously haven't taken their own advice. In response, atheists will usually try to define a moral code that most people would agree to, but this doesn't help matters.

Many atheists will say happiness is the standard for human behavior, but happiness varies from person to person. Adolph Hitler and Mother Theresa had different views on what it meant to be happy, so who was right? Other atheists claim morality is based on the idea that we shouldn't harm other people. While most people would agree, serial murderers, pedophiles, rapists and any number of common criminals would disagree. Since morality is just a matter of personal opinion, whose opinion is right? Besides, if life is all about 'survival of the fittest,' wouldn't harming people be good if it meant getting ahead in life? Surely if it makes a person more likely to pass their genes on to the next generation, it couldn't be considered a bad thing. Indeed, building a moral code around the belief we are here only to pass on our genes is troublesome. For example, if life is all about reproduction, why would rape be a bad thing? Rape generally increases the odds of passing genes on to the next generation, so why would an atheist have a problem with it? Sadly, many people have enforced moral codes based on the belief that we are only here to reproduce. The results have been tragic.

Atheists may not believe in Hell, but many atheist leaders have done their best to create Hell on earth. The 20th century was, by far, the bloodiest century in human history. Atheists such as Adolph Hitler, Joseph Stalin, Pol Pot and Mao Zedong murdered millions of people. Still, most atheists condemn their actions as immoral. Why do they believe their opinion to be superior? According to their own worldview, they have no right to be outraged. There is no right or wrong, after all, just personal preference. So why do so many atheists think what Hitler did was wrong? Could it be that human beings have consciences? If we do, it seems odd that they would've evolved. What good would a conscience be if only the 'fittest' survive to pass on their genes? Besides, where is this conscience? We can't observe it under a microscope. Does this mean the human conscience is, like thoughts, just a result of chemical reactions in the brain? For the atheist, it would have to be, because they believe the only things that exist are physical. So, if a person's conscience is determined by brain chemistry, there'd still be no reason to condemn Hitler for what he did. He shouldn't be held accountable for having insensitive atoms.

If this is true, this also means that there is no such thing as human dignity. Why would humans be of any more value than a blade of grass? For the atheist, they are both just arrangements of atoms. Actually, evolution teaches that the blade of grass and the human both came from the same one-celled organism. Since we supposedly share a common ancestor, why give preferential treatment to other humans? Additionally, there would be no use in talking about evil and suffering.

Those terms would be nothing more than a matter of personal opinion. Joseph Stalin and Mother Theresa had different definitions of evil and suffering, and neither definition could be considered right or wrong by an atheist. It's all up to personal interpretation, for better and for worse. Without God, and His absolute moral law, there is no right and wrong, no good and evil, no purpose, no plan, no freedom and no hope. Without God, life is meaningless.

What Comes Around Goes Around

While many people today have faith in evolution, few of them are willing to accept it completely. They just can't shake the feeling that there's more to life than passing their genes on to the next generation. To fill this spiritual void, a lot of individuals choose to believe the material world itself is divine. In other words, they believe everything is 'God.' Commonly known as pantheism, claiming that God is everything doesn't really tell us anything. Giving the universe a new name doesn't change the universe. It won't become something else because it has a new name. Besides, if 'God' really was the same as 'everything' this would make the Creator the same as His creation. Since God refers to the personal, eternal, almighty Creator of the universe, how could God also be the universe? How does an eternal being create Himself?

Clearly, like atheists, pantheists do not believe in an all-powerful Creator. Pantheists consider everything to be 'God.' Of course, if everything is 'God,' what difference is there between a blade of grass and a human being? What right would a human have to cut their lawn, if the lawn is just as 'divine' as a human being? Indeed, if everything is

'God' there is also no difference between right and wrong, good and evil. Murdering someone and trying to save a life would be exactly the same, because both actions are a part of 'God.' On top of that, why would a doctor's moral code be better than a serial murderer's? They are both 'God,' so whose opinion of right and wrong is more acceptable? Regardless, pantheism is quite common, with Buddhism being one of the more popular forms.

Buddhism

Buddhism is based on the teachings of Buddha, a gentleman who believed life consisted of immense suffering. This suffering was thought to be caused by human desire. Only removing desire, through meditation and good deeds, could release a person from their suffering. Buddha also believed life consisted of a continuous cycle of physical rebirths, with karma being the law by which everyone would be judged. Good karma, which comes from good deeds, leads to a person being reborn as a human being. This makes it more likely that a person will achieve enlightenment, which is the total removal of personal desire and suffering. Bad karma, which comes from actions that cause suffering, leads to a person being reborn as an animal. This is why vegetarianism is encouraged among many Buddhists. Naturally, being reborn as an animal makes it a lot harder to become enlightened. In order to eventually become humans again, people reborn as animals must behave well. Sadly, karma can't be forgiven and there aren't any exceptions. So, reincarnation is a continual process of birth, death and rebirth until a person becomes enlightened.

Of course, since Buddhists don't believe in God, how would karma work? If there is no God, there are no moral laws. What's right and wrong is decided by personal opinion. So, wouldn't good karma and bad karma just be a matter of personal opinion? Serial murderers would easily become enlightened, because to them, murder is good karma. Also, if there is no God, who is keeping track of all of this karma? Where exactly did the law of karma come from, if there is no Lawgiver? Without a Supreme Judge, who judges everyone's actions and sentences them to being reborn as an animal? On top of that, if people are somehow reincarnated as animals, then why don't animals behave better?

After all, to become human again, animals would have to be well-behaved. Yet, many animals survive by killing other animals. Insects regularly bite and sting humans. Killing, biting and stinging all cause suffering, so these animals are just storing up more bad karma for themselves. That said, if reincarnation is the worst that can happen, why not hurt other people? Murderers might turn into mosquitoes, but they can still work their way back to personhood. It might take awhile, but if a person really wants to kill someone, going to the back of the line might be worth it. With reincarnation, everyone gets unlimited chances. If this is true, however, why has the human population grown so much over the past couple of centuries? Since someone has to die to be reborn, and there were far fewer people in the past than there are now, who is being reincarnated to account for the current human population? As Buddhists don't believe in a Creator, no new souls can be created, so where are all the souls coming from? To add to the confusion, Buddhists don't believe human beings have a soul.[14] So, if people have no souls, what part of them is reincarnated? Surely it isn't their body. Souls or not, how did this cycle of reincarnation start in the first place? Clearly, a belief in reincarnation is problematic. Still, Buddhists are hardly the only group that believes in a cycle of birth, death and rebirth.

The More Things Change, the More They Stay the Same

If you've been watching daytime television lately, you've probably heard about the New Age Movement. While popular, the New Age Movement is nothing more than a giant rerun. There's nothing new about it. Several of the beliefs held by New Agers come from Hinduism, with multiple other ancient religions also shaping their doctrine. This melting pot of religious beliefs is based on the idea that "all religions lead to God." Naturally, if all religions lead to God, they must all have true information about God. So, all religions are true. This would mean Islam, for example, must be true. The problem, however, is that Islam teaches all non-Islamic religions are false. According to Islam, which New Agers believe is true, all religions aren't true. Some people might object by saying "all religions really just teach the same thing." Simply put, this is false. For example, Mormons believe in many gods, Muslims believe in one God, Buddhists claim everything is 'God' and atheists say there is no God. They can't all be right about who God is. There can't be many gods, one God and no God at the same time. Since various religions teach contradictory things, all religions can't be true. If all religions can't be true, they can't all lead to God, because only one of them has the right information about who God is. In other words, only one belief about God is true.

To get around this, many New Agers will say that "what's true for you isn't true for me." This might sound good at first, but it doesn't make a lot of sense. For starters, truth is what corresponds to reality. Truth is telling it like it is. If something is true, it describes the actual state of things. All truths are absolute. Even if I say I like the color blue more than the color yellow, it is absolutely true for everybody that I prefer the color blue to the color yellow. Beliefs can't change the truth. A person who sincerely believes the sum of 2+2 is 5 is still wrong. It doesn't matter what culture someone is from, the sum of 2+2 will always be 4 for everyone. Our beliefs about things might change, but the truth doesn't change. The earth always revolved around the sun, not just when people discovered this fact and began to believe it was true. So, if something is true for me, it's true for you.

After all, gravity doesn't play favorites. It's true for everybody, regardless of what people think about it. Besides, if what is true for one person really isn't true for another, what point would there be in teaching anyone about anything? It'd all be relative. If people think it's true Seattle is the capital city of Malawi, why tell them they're wrong? It's their 'truth.' What point would there be in arguing over anything? How can a person say any position another person holds is wrong, if what's true for one person isn't true for another? What point would there be in laws? If it's true for someone that murder is good, wouldn't laws against murder be discriminatory? Surely, laws against pedophilia, murder and rape would be mighty arrogant. Why should one person's 'truth' be better than another person's 'truth?'

Of course, even the New Age Movement embraces absolute truth. For example, the New Age Movement, Hinduism and Buddhism all teach a form of reincarnation. Hindus believe the human soul is reincarnated, while Buddhists don't believe humans have a soul at all. Well, New Agers believe humans have a soul. According to New Age teaching, then, Buddhists are wrong on this matter. Yet, since the New Age Movement teaches evolution, how can New Agers believe in the existence of the human soul? If the material world is all there is, as evolution claims, where'd the soul come from? The New Age Movement also teaches, like Buddhism and Hinduism, that everything is 'God.' New Agers often say "all is one." So, if everything is the same, why does each person have a unique soul?

Clearly, everybody has their own ideas, opinions and judgments. But if all is one, why would this be so? Why would one person have different memories from someone else, when everything and everyone is the same? If all is one, everyone should have the same memories. As if that weren't enough, the New Age Movement teaches everyone is 'God,' but people simply aren't aware of this and they need to be enlightened. According to New Agers, the next step in human evolution is for everyone to become one with the 'Force.' Only then will a 'New Age' of world peace be ushered in.

Just about everyone wants world peace, so how can the 'Force' be with you? Apparently, it takes a lot of hard work. To be at one with the universe, New Agers believe contact with 'higher spiritual beings' is a necessity. This requires the use of several occult practices, although the word occult is avoided at all costs. It's a 'negative energy' term. In plain English, it's bad for business. 'Spiritual self-improvement' is much more inviting. Unfortunately, the marketable makeover doesn't change the fact that astral projection, channeling and other New Age favorites are ancient occult classics.

Typically, the term occult refers to various practices which are used in an attempt to gain hidden knowledge or supernatural power apart from the God of the Bible. Since members of the New Age Movement reject the God of the Bible and must contact 'higher spiritual beings' to achieve enlightenment, they engage in several occult activities. For example, a number of New Agers turn to astral projection. This practice involves the training of the soul to leave the body and get in touch with entities from another dimension, or a different part of the universe. In addition to self-induced out-of-body experiences, New Agers are also prone to inviting spirit entities to possess them, an activity called channeling.

Needless to say, these occult practices assume spiritual forces and beings exist. Again, such an assumption is at odds with evolution. After all, if matter is all there is, why would the next step in human evolution be spiritual enlightenment? If evolution is true, there'd be no such thing as a spirit, a soul or a mind. To put it another way, astral projection wouldn't be much of a trip and channelers would get awfully lonely. Naturally, there'd be no 'higher spiritual beings' to guide us into a 'New Age.'

On the other hand, the Bible does speak of a spiritual dimension, but it's not at all like New Agers might imagine. Quite the opposite, the Bible speaks of spiritual warfare. Unlike New Age teaching, Jesus isn't just another 'ascended master' who was one with the 'Force.' On the contrary, the Bible says that "by him were all things created, that are in heaven, and that are in earth, visible and invisible, whether they be thrones, or dominions, or principalities, or powers: all things were created by him, and for him."[15] Jesus is the Creator of all things, including the unseen spiritual realm and the beings which inhabit it. These beings are called angels, and not all of them are good.[16]

This wasn't always the case. In the beginning all of the angels were good, but like humans, God created angels with free will. Some of them rebelled. Despite popular belief, angels aren't 'fairies' who float around on clouds and play harps. They are spirit beings created by God to carry out His purposes, in Heaven and on earth. While they are spirit beings,[17] they have the ability to appear in human form.[18] Indeed, the Bible notes people have even "entertained angels unawares."[19] In case you were wondering, they always appear as men, which makes several love songs quite awkward. The Bible also says angels are more powerful than human beings,[20] and warns that they aren't to be worshiped.[21] Only God can be worshiped, but this didn't sit well with all of the angels. One angel in particular, corrupted by pride, led the charge.[22]

Hardly a red guy with a tail and a pitchfork, Satan tried to kick God off of His throne. He wanted to be God, and he wasn't alone. A third of the angels joined him,[23] and God judged their rebellion against Him by barring them from Heaven.[24] Since then, Satan has become "the god of this world" who has "blinded the minds of them which believe not."[25] The little 'g' makes it obvious Satan is a false god, that is, he is the ruler of all those who choose to believe his lies. Put differently, Satan is constantly working to deceive the world into worshiping him, no pitchfork required. Incidentally, some of his oldest lies happen to be the major beliefs of the New Age Movement.

In the Garden of Eden, Satan tempted the first woman, Eve, to rebel against God.[26] Satan told Eve she wouldn't die if she disobeyed God.[27] This statement is similar to reincarnation, which teaches that nobody ever really dies. As a result, there's no need to worry if you rebel against God, because there aren't any eternal consequences for our actions. Next, in the day Eve chose to disobey God, Satan said her eyes would be opened and she would be like God.[28] Of course, the New Age Movement teaches we are all ignorant of our own divinity, and we all need to have our eyes opened. Well, Eve believed Satan. Clearly, it didn't bring about a 'New Age' of world peace. In fact, the Bible says it had the opposite effect.

Now, this doesn't mean Satan has free rein on earth. His power is limited because he's a created being. Satan can only do what God allows,[29] but this raises the question, "Why would God allow Satan to deceive people?" Simply put, God didn't create robots. Everyone has free will. Adam and Eve had the choice to obey Him, or believe Satan's deception. They liked the sound of Satan's deception more, so they chose to believe it. They freely disobeyed God. In so doing, they opened the door for the rest of us. God is no respecter of persons.[30] Like Adam and Eve, everyone must choose their allegiance. We all have the choice to obey God, or disobey Him by believing one of Satan's deceptions.

Fortunately, for those troubled by this news of spiritual warfare, there's no need to worry. The Bible says the battle was over before it started, and Jesus is victorious.[31] There will be more on that later. For the time being, it should be noted that Satan isn't going to be the ruler of Hell. Nothing could be further from the truth. Satan is going to be in Hell for eternity all right, but as its prisoner.[32] At the appointed time, he will meet this horrible end. Until then, Satan will continue roaming the earth "seeking whom he may devour."[33] To draw more people to his lies, he will keep disguising himself as "an angel of light."[34] After all, if his lies weren't appealing, why would anyone be deceived? With this in mind, it's not a surprise God strongly condemns occult practices.[35] Given the evil nature of Satan and his angels, also called demons, occult activities are highly dangerous. Out of love, God has outlawed these practices.

Besides, there should be no need for 'enlightenment' anyway. Indeed, if all is one, why doesn't everyone know they are 'God' already? If everyone and everything are the same, why would someone need to be convinced that everyone and everything is the same? Additionally, if everything is the same, what difference is there between a human being and a tree? What right would a human being have to cut a tree down, if they're both 'God'? If everything is the same, what point would there be in going to school, getting a job, or eating healthy? Being uneducated, poor and obese would be the same as being educated, rich and in good shape. If a person really wanted anything, though, the New Age Movement also teaches people can create their own reality.

If this were true, we would expect to find a lot more really good-looking billionaires. All kidding aside, this belief could be quite harmful. If a gentleman jumps off of a cliff and believes really hard he can fly, he isn't going to suddenly sprout wings. An equally dangerous belief held by New Agers is that reality is an illusion. For example, if a group of New Agers stumbled upon a drowning man, why would any of them bother trying to save him? The New Age Movement teaches the person is an illusion drowning in illusory water. It's not really happening. In addition, since everyone can create their own reality, this gentleman could just think a way out of the situation. If he does die, his soul will be reincarnated anyway, so why bother jumping in to help save his life?

Thankfully, reality isn't an illusion. We're all really here. Consider that if everything really was an illusion, how would we know this to be true? Since all of our thoughts would be illusions, we couldn't trust any of them. On top of that, if everything is an illusion, no one would know if any New Age beliefs were true. As we've seen, however, we can know for certain the beliefs of the New Age Movement are entirely false. They don't correspond to reality; they fail to describe the actual state of things. Still, the ancient beliefs that form the doctrine of the New Age Movement continue to gain widespread acceptance. Deep down, it seems many people would rather exchange the truth for a global religion that makes everyone feel better about themselves. Getting along is more important than the truth. The growth in popularity of age-old New Age doctrine is rivaled only by the belief that extraterrestrials are the real masterminds behind human existence.

Mars Attacks!

Long ago, in a galaxy…how does that go again? In all seriousness, many people take lines from science fiction movies quite seriously. These days, there is a growing number of people who believe extraterrestrials exist, and that these aliens created life on earth.[36] It is believed that an advanced race of aliens shipped some form of simple life to earth on spaceships, billions of years ago. Many 'earthlings' also maintain these aliens will return in the event of some kind of major disaster, such as an environmental catastrophe or an energy crisis. They will swoop in and be the saviors of humanity, possibly restoring the earth to mint condition. Other people think the aliens will transport them, in spaceships, to a different planet that is still in good shape. Of course, all of these beliefs are based on the assumption aliens exist in the first place. Assuming they do exist, why would they bother bringing microscopic life to earth? How could they know this organism would turn into a human being over billions of years? Granted, given the effects of natural selection and genetic mutations, they probably weren't expecting anything more than the microscopic organism they supposedly brought with them.

After all, spending billions of years waiting for humans to evolve seems highly unlikely for such an advanced race. Yet, if 'earthlings' did evolve from this one-celled organism that extraterrestrials brought to earth, where'd the extraterrestrials come from? Who made them? Most people believe non-living chemicals somehow gave rise to a one-celled organism on a distant planet, in spite of the Law of Biogenesis. So, the idea that aliens evolved from non-living chemicals is accepted by blind faith. While there has also never been any contact with an extraterrestrial, most people are quite certain the government isn't telling us the whole story.

This is a popular belief, but if the government had proof that aliens exist, why would they cover it up? Millions of taxpayer dollars were spent on NASA's Search for Extraterrestrial Intelligence (SETI) program, and the lack of results led to its cancellation. It would have been a good idea to justify the taxpayer expense by providing some evidence that the program wasn't a waste of time, but no such evidence existed. After the cancellation of NASA's program, numerous private SETI programs cropped up. To this day, none of them have found any signs of life 'out there' to wet the appetite of their financial backers. Such an amazing discovery would surely rake in more money for research, so it's quite clear they aren't hiding anything.

Still, the search continues. With the massive size of the universe, many people are convinced there must be life 'out there.' While the universe is definitely huge, this doesn't mean humans have company on a far away planet. Everyone is impressed by the extraordinary number of stars, planets and galaxies in the universe. It's by design. The Bible says "The heavens declare the glory of God."[37] Sure, a lot of people look up and think about what might be 'out there' instead of considering the Creator that made it all. Regardless, the astonishing size of the universe displays God's awesome power. How so?

Let's say you could travel at the speed of light. You would be traveling at approximately 186,000 miles per second, which is roughly 670 million miles per hour. You'll probably want to make sure your seatbelt is securely fastened, and your seatback and tray table are in their full upright and locked position. Now, traveling at the speed of light, you would cover 5.8 trillion miles in a year. That's a lot of frequent flyer miles, but unfortunately, you wouldn't get the chance to use them. Indeed, even at light speed, it would take approximately 100,000 years to travel across the Milky Way. To reach the next closest galaxy, Andromeda, it would take roughly 2,300,000 years.

Of course, it's theoretically impossible to accelerate anything with mass to the speed of light. According to Einstein's Special Theory of Relativity, the speed of light is the maximum speed an object with mass can go, because the faster it travels the greater its mass becomes. At the speed of light, its mass becomes infinite, and so does the energy needed to move it. Put differently, it would take an infinite amount of energy to propel an object with mass to the speed of light. Clearly, traveling at the speed of light isn't going to be happening anytime soon. Yet, even if it were a reality, it would only be fast enough for us to see a fraction of the Milky Way.

To boldly go where no man has gone before, we really need to exceed the speed of light. Since an object with mass can't travel as fast or faster than light speed, however, kicking it into 'warp drive' is easier said than done. Faster-than-light travel would require space itself to be folded in some way. A few suggestions for making this happen have been proposed, such as wormholes or exotic propulsion mechanisms, but they all remain highly speculative. To put it mildly, traveling millions of light years in a few hours is light on the science and heavy on the fiction.

In response, a lot of people assume an advanced race of extraterrestrials could've easily developed the technology to travel faster than the speed of light. In fact, unidentified flying objects are often held as proof that aliens are visiting us all the time. Although many people think of UFOs as flying saucers operated by little green men, no part of a flying saucer has ever been recovered. Due to the lack of concrete evidence, UFO researchers rely on eyewitness accounts. Organizations such as the Center for UFO Studies, the Mutual UFO

Network and the National UFO Reporting Center routinely investigate incidents. For the most part, UFO sightings which aren't hoaxes can be explained by natural phenomena. Some of the more commonly mistaken objects include Venus, weather balloons, lenticular clouds and meteors. As a result, a lot of people disregard UFO sightings altogether, but there are a few incidents which aren't as easy to dismiss. Does this mean we're being visited by extraterrestrials?

The late Dr. J. Allen Hynek, an astrophysicist and one of the best-respected UFO investigators in the world, didn't think so. The founder of the Center for UFO Studies, Hynek maintained UFOs were from another dimension, not another galaxy. He was far from alone. He and his well-known protégé Dr. Jacques Vallée observed "If UFOs are, indeed, somebody else's "nuts and bolts hardware," then we must still explain how such tangible hardware can change shape before our eyes." They added, "We must wonder too, where UFOs are "hiding" when not manifesting themselves to human eyes."[38] Curiously, UFOs have been picked up on radar, but they've never been detected entering the earth's atmosphere. With so many UFO sightings, how could such a large number of alien spaceships be secretly entering and leaving our atmosphere?

Besides, the earth is an extremely small part of the universe. Why would it be the recipient of so much attention? To add to the mystery, UFOs appear to be physical entities, but they don't obey the laws of physics. Another highly-regarded UFO investigator, John Keel, pointed out they can "execute impossible maneuvers, such as sudden right angle turns, and disappear as mysteriously as they had come."[39] With this evidence in mind, Keel, by no means a Christian, concluded

"UFO manifestations seem to be, by and large, merely minor variations of the age-old demonological phenomenon."[40] Is this a reasonable conclusion?

All in all, there are only three possible explanations for UFOs. First, UFO sightings can be dismissed altogether. Some of them are hoaxes, and most of the other incidents can be explained by natural phenomena. What about the few unsolved cases? Well, they can be treated like unsolved homicides. There just isn't enough evidence to determine what went down. On top of that, in a culture saturated with science fiction, can the eyewitness accounts really be trusted? Of course, this doesn't seem to account for UFOs being picked up on radar or incidents where pilots have fired upon them. Despite being detected and fired at, no UFO has ever been captured or shot down. It appears that something is going on, and there's more to it than meets the eye.

To explain what's happening, many people are quick to suggest UFOs are advanced alien spacecraft. This explanation for UFO sightings requires several assumptions. For starters, extraterrestrials would have to exist. Next, they would've had to develop the ability to travel faster than the speed of light. Finally, they would have to somehow be capable of operating machinery which can morph in mid-flight and execute physics-defying maneuvers. The likelihood of all these assumptions being true isn't very good. So, many renowned researchers like Hynek, Vallée and Keel determined UFOs came from another dimension, and were a modern manifestation of age-old activity.

For instance, modern 'alien abduction' testimonies sound awfully similar to ancient stories involving demons. Keel was particularly struck by the similarities, noting "Victims of demonomania (possession) suffer the very same medical and emotional symptoms as the UFO contactees." He added "Strange objects and entities materialize and dematerialize in these stories, just as the UFOs and their splendid occupants appear and disappear, walk through walls, and perform other supernatural feats."[41] Now, personal testimonies about being abducted lack physical evidence, so most people are quick to conclude these events have a medical or psychological explanation. The late John Mack, a famous abduction researcher and one-time Harvard Professor of Psychiatry, disagreed. In an interview, he observed "It's both literally, physically happening to a degree; and it's also some kind of psychological, spiritual experience occurring and originating perhaps in another dimension."[42] In other words, he didn't believe alien spaceships were beaming people up.

On the contrary, Mack's description is quite consistent with what the Bible says about Satan and his angels, also known as demons. All angels, good and bad, are powerful spiritual beings that can appear physically. God created them with the ability to cause both visions[43] and dreams.[44] These visions and dreams can be very real to the bodily senses, but they do not physically occur. Throughout the Bible, good angels gave messages through dreams and visions, or they delivered messages in person while appearing as men. Angels can also cause events to physically happen. On one occasion, a good angel freed a follower of Jesus, named Peter, from prison.[45] The angel caused Peter's chains to fall off and opened an iron gate without touching it, before suddenly disappearing. During the jail-break, Peter was in a trance-like state. He thought he was having a vision, but to his pleasant surprise, he had been busted out of prison in style.

Unfortunately, Satan and his angels can cause visions and dreams too, and they use them to communicate false information. They hate God, and want nothing more than to keep people from a true knowledge of Him. To accomplish this task, they use visions and dreams to communicate deceptive messages. Their goal is to convince people of their lies, so these individuals will go around spreading the false information as if it were the truth. This deceives more people into worshiping their lies, and it keeps people from a true knowledge of God and His love for them. Jesus called Satan the father of lies for a reason.[46] When it comes to lying, Satan is the best there is. Naturally, for a lie to be believed, it has to appear credible.

In the distant past, people claimed to have encounters with 'goblins,' 'elves' or 'fairies' of some kind. Back then, it was culturally acceptable to believe in these mythological creatures. These days, it's culturally acceptable to believe in extraterrestrials. Since Satan and his angels are deceptive, it only makes sense they would do their best to fit in with the popular folklore of the day. That said, their behavior really hasn't changed. Some 'abduction' testimonies are downright disturbing, and they share a lot in common with ancient accounts involving demons. In the words of Jacques Vallée, "The 'medical examination' to which abductees are said to be subjected, often accompanied by sadistic sexual manipulation, is reminiscent of the medieval tales of encounters with demons."[47] Unsurprisingly, religious beliefs play a big role in who experiences abductions.

Speaking of people who report being abducted, Harvard Professor of Psychology Richard McNally observed "Most of them had pre-existing new-age beliefs – they were into bio-energetic therapies, past lives, astral projection, tarot cards, and so on."[48] While New Age beliefs are common among people who experience these events, there's one set of beliefs that isn't. Joe Jordan and Wes Clark, co-founders of the CE-4 Research Group, have spent years analyzing abduction accounts. In the course of their research, Clark noticed "The Christians reporting the abduction experience tended to be people who intellectually espoused the existence of God, but didn't apply it personally. But there seemed to be an obvious absence of devout, Bible believing, "walk the walk" Christians."[49] Apparently, the 'abductors' have discriminating taste. What's more, Clark added "As the number of cases mounted, the data showed that in every instance where the victim knew to invoke the name of Jesus Christ, the event stopped."[50]

Sadly, despite the horrifying nature of these experiences, there are some people who don't want them to end. Whitley Strieber is one of them. Mr. Strieber, who holds several New Age beliefs, is one of the more famous abductees around. He's written a couple of popular books on his encounters with what he calls 'visitors.' In fact, through the occult practice of channeling, he has invited these 'visitors' to possess him. This event is often called a 'walk-in' in New Age circles, but that's just a nicer way of saying demon possession. Even Strieber once admitted "I wondered if I might not be in the grip of demons, if they were not making me suffer for their own purposes, or simply for their enjoyment."[51] Since the messages they've given him are quite anti-biblical, this seems like a reasonable conclusion. After all, as researchers

John Ankerberg and John Weldon pointed out "how credible is it to think that literally thousands of genuine extraterrestrials would fly millions or billions of light years simply to teach New Age philosophy, deny Christianity, and support the occult?" It doesn't seem likely. The gentlemen went on to say "And why would the entities actually possess and inhabit people (as in Walk-ins and channeling) just like demons do if they were really advanced extraterrestrials?"[52] Clearly, these beings aren't from outer space.

Ultimately, the Bible doesn't say God created extraterrestrials. It also doesn't tell us to ever expect contact with them, so it's safe to say they aren't around. On the other hand, it does tell us to expect visitors of another sort. The Bible says that "in the latter times some shall depart from the faith, giving heed to seducing spirits, and doctrines of devils."[53] The Bible speaks of a spiritual dimension, and demons are a part of this dimension. All things considered, UFOs and so-called abductions are consistent with what the Bible says about demonic deception. The suggestion of a spiritual dimension is often ignored, however, because such an immaterial explanation would confirm the existence of the God of the Bible.

Immaterial

From an early age, all of us were taught that we were living in a material world. This was presented as an obvious fact of life. We were trained to think the universe created itself by chance. It was a certainty that non-living chemicals formed into a living organism with complex genetic information. Natural selection, a mechanism which reduces genetic information, surely made this one-celled organism more complex over millions of years. But, how many hands went up in class to ask, how do you know? If this question had been asked, how could someone that believes in evolution possibly respond?

After all, evolution is a theory of history based on the assumption that matter is all there is. If this assumption is true, all of our thoughts are simply the result of chemical reactions in the brain. Why trust them? Indeed, there'd be no logical reason to accept any 'thoughts.' According to evolution itself, there's no logical reason to accept evolution. To be fair, if all 'thoughts' are predetermined by the makeup of our brain, people who believe in evolution can't even help their belief in it. They have no mind of their own, for they have no mind at all. Often, however, a person will claim that they accept evolution because it is 'scientific.'

In reality, it takes an extraordinary leap of faith to believe in evolution. It is assumed that, in the beginning, nothing created matter. This violates the First Law of Thermodynamics, a principle scientific law, which states matter and energy can't be created or destroyed. After this, the matter somehow made itself expand, in spite of the scientific Law of Inertia. Since everything that has a beginning has a cause, what set these events in motion? Usually, the answer is chance, although chance can't cause an event to happen. Chance refers to mathematical probabilities, or odds. It can't make anything actually occur. So, it is believed that nothing created the universe.

Sometime later, evolution teaches non-living chemicals created a living organism. This violates the scientific Law of Biogenesis, which states living organisms can only come from other living organisms. Despite this hurdle, it is believed this organism also had DNA, an elegant and complex information storage system. This violates the First and Second scientific Laws of Information. Matter can't create non-material entities, and information is a non-material entity. Additionally, DNA needs an intricate molecular machine known as a ribosome to decode it, but the instructions to build ribosomes are on the DNA. Which came first, the DNA or the ribosome? Regardless, it is thought that natural selection made this one-celled organism more complex, in spite of the fact natural selection doesn't create genetic information. It's natural selection, not natural creation. The mechanism selects from existing information. Over time, natural selection reduces genetic information. Since the selection process does the opposite of what evolution requires, copying mistakes in genetic code are sometimes believed to have given rise to new information. On the contrary, genetic mutations corrupt existing information. They may create new traits, including many well-known disorders, but mutations don't lead to new genetic information.

Quite clearly, people who believe in evolution accept all of these assumptions, many of which violate scientific laws, by faith. Of course, there is a measure of faith in any theory of history. Recall there are two types of science, experimental and historical. While many people confuse the two, evolution is clearly a historical science, because it attempts to figure out how we all got here. Well, history can't be repeated and no one can directly experiment on past events. Any explanation about the past requires assumptions. Since everyone has biases, our assumptions about the past are going to be different depending on what we believe about why we're here.

Christians believe in the God of the Bible. The biblical account of creation is an eyewitness account of how everyone got here. On the other hand, a person who believes in evolution denies there is an eternal, infinite Creator of the universe. Evolution is based on the assumption that the material world, or nature, is all there is. Some people might claim immaterial entities such as the mind and the soul exist, but they are being inconsistent with their belief in evolution.

So, it is not a debate over science and faith. Rather, it is a choice between two theories of history, both of which must be accepted by faith. Which faith is more reasonable? Is it reasonable to believe the universe is self-created? How does something that doesn't exist create itself? Is it rational to believe nothing created everything by chance? How does nothing, the absence of something, create anything? Which faith is supported by observations from the experimental sciences? Evolution violates numerous scientific laws, but if evolution is actually true, why would experimental science work at all?

Experimental science, which has led to advancements in areas such as medicine and technology, involves conducting controlled, repeatable experiments in the here and now. But, if the world around us is a result of random, highly unlikely accidents, why would we expect there to be predictable outcomes for experiments? Why would the universe be orderly at all? Why would there be laws governing nature? It's hard to imagine these laws evolved over time. Which laws came first, and are they still evolving? It's hard to believe gravity would cease to exist someday. On top of this, why would we trust anyone's interpretations of an experiment's results?

The results of an experiment must be interpreted. Data doesn't interpret itself. Yet, if our thoughts are just the result of chemical reactions in the brain, why would we trust the findings of an experiment to be logically sound? The interpretations would follow the laws of chemistry, not the laws of logic. In fact, why would logic exist at all? It certainly isn't a material entity. Not only could we not trust the findings of an experiment, there would also be no reason to report the results of an experiment honestly. If evolution is true, lying wouldn't be right or wrong, so why not fabricate a cure for cancer to obtain more research money? Without a doubt, evolution provides no foundation for morality, logic, science and free-will. It isn't consistent with the world around us. So, why is it that so many people believe in evolution?

Philosopher Michael Ruse once stated "Evolution is a religion. This was true of evolution in the beginning, and it is true of evolution still today."[54] People choose to believe in evolution not because it is true, but because they don't want God to exist. Philosophy professor Thomas Nagel admitted "I want atheism to be true and am made uneasy by the fact that some of the most intelligent and well informed people I know are religious believers. It isn't just that I don't believe in God and naturally, hope there is no God! I don't want there to be a God; I don't want the universe to be like that."[55] If there is no God, life has no meaning. This sounds pretty depressing, but it also means we aren't responsible for our actions. No one is accountable for what they do. Nobody has to follow God's rules. Everyone makes up their own rules.

Atheist Aldous Huxley, author of *Brave New World* and other works, acknowledged he "had motive for not wanting the world to have a meaning." Why? Huxley explained "the philosophy of meaninglessness was essentially an instrument of liberation from a certain system of morality. We objected to the morality because it interfered with our sexual freedom."[56] If there's no God, there's no right and wrong, so anything goes. Mass murderer Jeffrey Dahmer once said "If a person doesn't think there is a God to be accountable to, then—then what's the point of trying to modify your behavior to keep it within acceptable ranges? That's how I thought anyway. I always believed the theory of evolution as truth, that we all just came from the slime. When we, when we died, you know, that was it, there is nothing."[57] Now, why were Mr. Huxley's drunken orgies acceptable, but Mr. Dahmer's murders worthy of punishment? If right and wrong is decided by human opinion, why would murder be wrong? Also, if human actions are the result of chemical reactions in the brain, how can people be held accountable for their behavior?

Quite frankly, Dahmer's defense team blew it. Why didn't Dahmer's lawyers tell him to say "My atoms made me do it!" This may sound absurd, but it is consistent with what evolution teaches. Since many people find the existence of God uncomfortable, they'll accept anything to remove Him from their lives. They'll believe the universe is self-created, nothing created everything and non-living chemicals created life. In other words, the truth is immaterial. The truth doesn't matter. This is why so many people compromise their position on evolution to add purpose to their life.

It's the best of both worlds, or so it seems. People are comforted by the idea there is some kind of meaning to life, but they don't like the fact God tells them what to do. So, people turn to religions which claim 'God' is everything. All this does, however, is change the definition of the word 'God' to mean everything. There is still no belief in a personal, eternal Creator that holds us all accountable for our wrongdoing. Put simply, either God created everything, or everything created itself. If everything created itself, matter is all there is. There would be no God. So, if there's no God, there can be no soul, no mind, no freedom, no good and evil, no right and wrong, and no life after death of any kind. There isn't a middle ground. It's either one or the other. Religions like Buddhism, Hinduism and the New Age Movement contradict evolution. Since they can't consistently explain how we got here, how can they explain why we're here?

Now, from time to time, people who have put their hope in evolution have doubts. What if the truth is important? What if being wrong has consequences? The Lord Jesus Christ taught that those who reject Him will be thrown "into a furnace of fire" where "there shall be wailing and gnashing of teeth."[58] Certainly, if evolution is true, it doesn't matter what you believe. Eat, drink and be merry, because when you die, the party is over. It all fades to black, and you're forever separated from everything you enjoy and everyone you love. How do you know? You can't. You haven't died yet, so you can't know for sure. So, what if you're wrong? What if there is eternal conscious torment for everyone who rejects Jesus Christ? You're going to be dead for a long time. The truth is worth a look.

The Gospel Truth

The Word of God

Despite being exiled to church pews and hotel room nightstands, the Holy Bible continues to be the best-selling book worldwide year-in and year-out. This may have a little something to do with the Bible's claim in 2 Timothy 3:16 that "All scripture is given by inspiration of God."[1] Inspiration doesn't mean human wisdom or 'enlightenment.' The Bible has one author: God. Approximately 40 men from a variety of backgrounds were guided by God so all of the words they recorded were without error. Inspiration also doesn't mean the writers were robots. They drew upon their experiences and used their own styles. Yet, God directed their thoughts, and He made sure they wrote exactly what He wanted in the exact way He wanted it written.

Now, God isn't directly involved every single time the Bible is copied. God inspired the original writers of the 66 books of the Bible, so the original writings are God-given. Does this mean we can't trust copies of the original writings? According to the late biblical scholar F.F. Bruce, "The evidence for our New Testament writings is ever so much greater than the evidence for many writings of classical authors, the authenticity of which no-one dreams of questioning."[2] Indeed, many ancient documents have only a handful of copies in existence.

Most of these copies were made hundreds of years after the original writings, making them more likely to have errors. On the other hand, there are roughly 24,000 copies of New Testament writings, some of which are dated within 100 years of the original documents.[3]

Since there are so many copies of the New Testament, they can all be cross-examined for consistency. The internal consistency of the New Testament writings is over 99%.[4] What about the small differences? Greek scholar D.A Carson concluded "The purity of text is of such a substantial nature that nothing we believe to be true, and nothing we are commanded to do, is in any way jeopardized by the variants."[5] In other words, even non-Christian scholars accept the New Testament's textual reliability. If they didn't, they would have to reject every other writing of the ancient world.

Clearly, the books of the New Testament haven't been changed, but how do we know the right books are in included in the Bible? For starters, a book had to be written by an apostle of Jesus Christ or a close associate of an apostle. For example, the Gospel of Mark was written by Mark. Mark wasn't an apostle, but he was a close associate of Peter, who was an apostle. Many people wrote false gospels and letters, pretending they were written by an apostle. Of course, the false writings were easy to spot because they were written well after any of the apostles were alive. The Gospel of Judas is a famous case. Judas didn't write the Gospel of Judas. He was dead a long time before the book was even written. Why then would someone pretend to be Judas? Put simply, it was 'reverse-plagiarism.' The person pretending to be an apostle wanted to give their teachings credibility by putting an apostle's name on it. The false teachings of these counterfeits conflicted greatly with the books that were written by the apostles and their close associates. This made it that much easier for Christians to recognize the false writings as fakes.

Certainly, God's Word was recognized by Christians. No organization or council decided what books would be included in the Bible. No group of humans gave the world the Bible. On the contrary, the books in the Holy Bible were given by God and they were recognized as God's Word by early Christians. Humans didn't decide what God's Word was; they discovered what God's Word was. Later councils confirmed the authoritative list of books that had already been recognized and used by early Christians for years. They didn't add or subtract any books.[6] Naturally, since the entire Bible is God-given, it is completely accurate in every part. Some people will point out that the Bible records people's lies, but the lies they told are reported accurately in the Bible. The Bible is a perfectly true account of everything it records as having taken place.

Although the Bible claims to be the Word of God, many people aren't impressed. What's in a claim? After all, every time we say "I felt" or "I dreamt" we are asking for other people to take our word for it. While people frequently lie, God cannot.[7] He is perfect, and so He is perfectly reliable. The Bible claims to be the Word of God. It's either true or false. If the Bible isn't the Word of God, you can let it collect dust in the hotel room nightstand. But, what if you're wrong? Surely, if the Bible is truly the written Word of God, it has the answer to the 'why' question. So, how do Christians know the Bible is God's Word?

Consistency

There isn't a book out there quite like the Holy Bible. The Bible contains numerous literary styles, such as history, poetry and proverbs. It was written in Hebrew, Aramaic and Greek from all over the continents of Europe, Asia and Africa. Not only did many of the writers never meet, but they also came from a wide variety of backgrounds. The writers of the Bible included fishermen, shepherds, kings, a doctor and a tax collector, among others. They also wrote under different circumstances. Paul wrote from various prisons throughout the Roman Empire, while Solomon wrote from his Jerusalem palace. In addition, the writers had completely different purposes for writing. Isaiah warned Israel of God's coming judgment, while Paul instructed several Christian churches in Europe and Asia. Still, despite being written over roughly 1,600 years by approximately 40 writers, all 66 books of the Bible are organized around the same theme: God's redemption of mankind. To say the least, this is not what we would expect to find. The writers of the various books address the 'who am I, where did I come from and why am I here' questions, and their answers don't conflict at all. On the contrary, they cover the existence of God, the creation of the world, mankind's rebellion against God and God's plan of redemption for the world without a single contradiction.

Let's recap. The Bible was written over a period of 1,600 years by roughly 40 writers from multiple walks of life. They wrote in different languages and on different continents. They wrote to different audiences, with different purposes and under different circumstances.

They made use of different literary forms, and amazingly, most of these writers never met each other. When all of the books were assembled together, we would expect the final product to be an unconnected and confused mess. Yet, we find the exact opposite. The Bible is one consistent, unfolding record of God's dealings with mankind, without a single contradiction. That's pretty extraordinary.

Honesty

The Bible is brutally honest. It tells it like it is. Where did death and suffering come from? It entered the world through the rebellion of Adam and Eve. Are humans basically good? Not according to the Bible. The Bible says the "heart is deceitful above all things, and desperately wicked."[8] The "imagination of man's heart is evil from his youth"[9] and "there is not a just man upon earth."[10] The people of the Bible, even those who did God's will, provide plenty of evidence to back up these observations. King David was a murderer and an adulterer,[11] Paul persecuted Christians,[12] Jacob was a liar[13] and Moses was a murderer.[14] Why would a group of men, often writing about people they admired, include all of these details? Some of the writers, such as Paul, Moses and Peter, wrote about their own faults. Why didn't they lie? They could've at least left the bad parts out. On top of that, why would a group of men write a book that paints mankind in such a negative light? Regardless, the human evil recorded in the Bible stands in sharp contrast to God's holiness, and His mercy towards mankind. The Bible doesn't honor humans; the Bible honors God.

Prophecy

When it comes to predicting the future, the Holy Bible is unmatched. For example, the books in the Old Testament contain a large number of predictions about the first coming of Jesus Christ. Despite being written many hundreds of years before Jesus Christ was born, all of them were fulfilled. Many of these prophecies spoke of His crucifixion. Psalm 22:16 foretold that Jesus Christ would be pierced in His hands and feet.[15] Zechariah 13:6 foretold that He would have wounds in His hands.[16] Amazingly, these predictions were made hundreds of years before Romans had refined the method of crucifixion to kill people. Of course, Jesus was crucified,[17] but the Old Testament also accurately predicted He would: be born in Bethlehem,[18] be born of a virgin,[19] be presented with gifts at birth,[20] be preceded by a prophet who would prepare His way,[21] teach in parables,[22] be hated without a cause,[23] heal the sick,[24] enter Jerusalem on a donkey,[25] be betrayed by a close friend who would eat with Him,[26] be betrayed for 30 pieces of silver,[27] be beaten,[28] be spat upon,[29] be humiliated,[30] be buried in a rich man's tomb[31] and have His clothing divided among His persecutors,[32] His side pierced[33] and none of His bones broken.[34] The Old Testament also accurately foretold His Resurrection.[35]

These are only a few of the fulfilled predictions the Old Testament made about Jesus Christ. In other words, there's plenty more where that came from. In addition, the Bible has also accurately predicted the future of nations several times. For example, Isaiah 66:8 foretold that the nation of Israel would be reborn – in one day.[36] This came to pass on May 14th, 1948, over two thousand years after Isaiah predicted it would happen and well over a thousand years since Israel had been a nation. What's the likelihood of hundreds of highly specific predictions about the future coming true? Let's just say it's not likely.

History

Overwhelmingly, archaeology confirms the history of the Bible. Archaeology is the scientific study of ancient peoples, through artifacts, fossils and other remains, to understand how these ancient civilizations lived. What do archaeologists think of the Bible? Archaeologist Clifford Wilson called the Bible "the ancient world's most reliable history textbook."[37] Archaeologist William Albright noted "Discovery after discovery has established the accuracy of innumerable details, and has brought increased recognition to the value of the Bible as a source of history."[38] For example, many people used to question the existence of Pontius Pilate, the Prefect of Judea at the time of Jesus. That all changed when archaeologists stumbled upon the Pilate Stone. The limestone block mentions the dedication of a building in honor of Tiberius Caesar Augustus by one "Pontius Pilate prefect of Judea." Still, with the many people and events recorded in the Bible, people often assume there must be at least one definite contradiction between archaeological evidence and the Bible. As professor of Hebrew and Semitic studies Keith Schoville put it "Thus far, no historical statement in the Bible has been proven false on the basis of evidence retrieved through archaeological research."[39] Instead, archaeology confirms the Bible's historical accuracy in many areas.[40]

Science

For the most part, people think experimental science and the Bible are at odds with one another. This couldn't be further from the truth. The Bible accurately describes the circulation of the atmosphere,[41] rock erosion,[42] the hydrologic cycle,[43] evaporation,[44] hydrothermal vents,[45] the importance of blood,[46] sea currents,[47] and living things reproducing after their kind.[48] These observations were made thousands of years before the scientific establishment caught on. The Bible also contains many health regulations about quarantining,[49] waste disposal,[50] burying the dead[51] and care for wounds and bodily discharges.[52] These rules were put in place thousands of years before humans had any understanding about bacteria. It's hard to believe the writers of the Bible knew more about modern medicine and science than the rest of the human race for thousands of years.

Power

The Bible is indestructible. It's been banned and burned, but it is available in more languages than any other book. Has any book influenced the world like the Bible? Despite the persecution of Christians throughout the years, it is the most well-known and widely-read book in human history. Surely, if the New Testament writings were false, the Roman government would've produced any evidence they could to stop the growth of Christianity. They didn't produce any. The New Testament was written and read by people that lived through the very events the New Testament recorded. No one, not even the enemies of Christianity, said the writings were made up.

Still, the Roman government routinely killed Christians. Why would they die for something that was made up? Why would they make something up knowing they would die? After all, few atheists would be willing to die for the cause of atheism. So why did they lay down their lives? Put simply, the message of the Bible changes lives. No book lifts more people up from lives of pain and suffering. No book offers more hope. No book is a more reliable account of how we got here and why we're here, for the Bible is truly the Word of God.

Creation

The only way to know what happened in the past, for sure, is to have a reliable eyewitness account. The Bible is that account. In the first chapter of Genesis, the first book of the Bible, God tells us He created everything in 6 days. On the first day, God created four things: time, space, matter and light. The Bible says "In the beginning, God created the heaven and the earth."[53] Before this, there was no time, space or matter. Only God existed. After creating these things, God created light.[54] He separated the light from the darkness, calling the light "Day" and the darkness "Night."[55]

Now, this light wasn't the sun. God didn't make the sun until the fourth day. You might be asking, "How could there be a day without the sun?" Well, a 24-hour day only requires the earth rotating on its axis. To distinguish between morning and evening, however, light also must be coming from one direction. In Genesis 1:3, God created a source of light. So, the earth was rotating in space and there was light coming from one direction. This was the first 24-hour day. On the second 24-hour day, God made the earth's atmosphere.[56] On the third day, God caused the waters of the earth to gather into the seas, so that dry land appeared. Then, He commanded the land to produce plants and trees.[57] During the fourth day, God created the sun, the moon and the stars. He made these not only to give light, but also to mark seasons, years and days.[58] God reserved the fifth day for creating the animals that live in the water and those that fly in the air.[59] Finally, on the sixth day, God made all of the land animals and the first human beings.[60]

In the second chapter of Genesis, we get more details on the creation of Adam and Eve. God made Adam from the dust of the earth and gave him rule over creation, including the authority to name certain animals.[61] Of course, Adam didn't have to name all of the animals, just the cattle, birds and land vertebrates.[62] He also didn't have to track them down. God brought the animals to him.[63] Still, you may be wondering, "How could Adam name all of the cattle, birds and land vertebrates in less than a day?"

For starters, Adam only had to name the original animal 'kinds,' not all of the 'species' we see today. Adam didn't have to name wolves, coyotes and poodles; he just had to name the dog kind. You might ask, "Isn't the existence of different species today proof of evolution?" Actually, this is natural selection, which does the opposite of what evolution requires. The process selects from existing genetic information and, over time, this reduces the information in a population. Originally, God created animal kinds with a wide variety of genetic information. Their genes were perfect, with no mutations. Since these original kinds had such genetic variety, their descendants could adapt to many different environments if they had to. This became very important when Adam and Eve's sin brought death and suffering into the world. Unfortunately, once certain genetic information is lost, it doesn't come back into a population. A poodle can't turn into a wolf or a coyote. The information has been bred out of the poodle population.

Clearly, then, Adam didn't have to name every species of cattle, bird and land vertebrate, just their various kinds. At most, he was naming a couple thousand animals. That still may sound difficult, but Adam was more than up to the task. He was created physically and mentally perfect. It wouldn't have been any trouble for Adam to name the animals God brought to him in only a few hours.[64]

After naming these animals, it became obvious Adam needed a companion. So, God caused Adam to fall into a deep sleep and He removed one of Adam's ribs. With Adam's rib, God made Eve.[65] Over the years, some people have wondered, "Why don't men have a missing rib then?" Well, if a dad lost one of his thumbs in an accident, would his children be born missing a thumb also? Certainly, they'd all be born with their thumbs intact. The genetic information to build thumbs is passed on from parents to their children. Removing a thumb, or a rib, wouldn't change any of the genes that are passed down. As a result, Adam didn't pass on his missing rib. Besides, Adam wasn't short a rib for very long.

After all, as any thoracic surgeon will tell you, ribs can grow back. Thoracic surgeons, also known as chest surgeons, regularly remove ribs. If the rib is carefully taken out of its periosteum, a membrane that lines the rib bone, the rib bone usually grows back. So, God chose from Adam the one bone that would completely grow back. While Adam was down a rib for a little while, He was still physically perfect because it grew back in a short time. At the end of the sixth day, God looked down and called His creation "very good."[66] There was no death, pain or suffering of any kind. Adam and Eve were even vegetarians, eating only plants and seeds.[67] On the seventh day, God stopped His work of creation.[68]

At this point, many people say "The word 'day' has lots of different meanings, so couldn't God have created everything in more than six 24-hour days?" God is infinite. He could've created everything in 6 seconds if He wanted to. Yet, the Holy Bible is quite clear, God created everything in six 24-hour days. Not only is each day numbered, but each of the first six days has an evening and a morning.[69] These days were not indefinite periods of time. God created everything in six 24-hour days. The real question to ask, then, is why did God take so long?

Most people know the earth's rotation on its axis, with one rotation taking about 24 hours, is the basis for a day. Many people are aware that the moon's shadow cycle, going from full moon to full moon, is the basis for a month. A complete cycle of phases takes roughly 30 days. Just about everybody knows the earth's trip around the sun, which takes approximately 365 days, is the basis for a year. What's the basis for a week? As Exodus 20:11 puts it, "in six days the Lord made heaven and earth, the sea, and all that in them is, and rested the seventh day."[70] There is no 7-day cycle in nature that would give us any idea of what a week is. Indeed, God chose to create everything in six days and rest on the seventh day to give us the basis for our week. Only the biblical account of creation provides the explanation, as it also does with the age of the earth.

'Billions and Billions of Years'

Most people use the expression 'billions and billions of years' as an exaggeration. When it comes to the age of the earth, however, people are dead serious when they talk about billions and billions of years. While it is widely believed that the earth is billions of years old, only God was there when the earth was formed. Since history can't repeat itself, any calculations about how old the earth is require assumptions about the past. People who believe in evolution assume matter is all there is. So, they believe the earth has to be billions of years old, in order to give the universe enough time to create itself. In other words, the universe couldn't have been made in six days by an infinite Creator, because they have faith God doesn't exist. People who believe in the biblical account of creation believe the earth is young, about 6,000 years old. Why only a few thousand years?

Well, there are very detailed genealogies in the Bible. These biblical genealogies show that Adam was created about 4000 B.C. and this was on the sixth day of creation. You might be wondering "How could the earth be approximately 6,000 years old, when scientific dating methods give dates of millions of years?" For starters, scientists don't have 'age-meters' they plug into rocks, and fossils certainly don't come with dates stamped on them. The age of a fossil is an example of historical science, so the 'dating game' involves a lot of assumptions. For instance, if you stumbled upon a burning candle, how would you determine how long it had been burning before you found it?[71] Sure, you could take the current height of the candle and the rate at which the candle is burning, but what would that tell you? You'd have to assume the candle has always burned at the same rate and what the starting height of the candle was to guess how long the candle had been burning. Your answer would change depending on the assumptions you make.

These assumptions, and others, apply to all radiometric dating methods. For example, with carbon dating, scientists assume the amount of carbon-14 in the atmosphere has always been constant and the carbon-14 decay rate hasn't changed. What's carbon-14? Without sounding too stuffy, carbon-14 forms from cosmic rays acting on nitrogen in the atmosphere. All living things have carbon-14 in them, but when living things die, the carbon-14 in their bodies begins to break down because it returns to nitrogen. Scientists make their starting assumptions, and then measure this carbon-14 to work out how old a dead organism might be. Of course, carbon-14 has a half-life of about 5,730 years. In plain English, this means roughly every 5,730 years, half of the carbon-14 in a dead organism decays away. Anything over approximately 50,000 years old shouldn't have any detectable carbon-14 left in it. In other words, if a sample contains carbon-14 in it, it is actually good evidence the sample isn't millions of years old. So, when someone tries to 'prove' something is millions of years old with carbon dating, they are trying to do the impossible. Something that old wouldn't have any carbon-14 in it.[72]

Unsurprisingly, with other radiometric dating methods, scientists who believe in evolution make assumptions which give them old ages. Although they assume millions of years are required for natural processes, this isn't consistent with scientific observation. After the eruption of Mount Saint Helens in 1980, the Toutle River was blocked by deposits of volcanic ash and debris. A couple of years later, a mudflow breached the area and eroded a canyon system up to 140 feet deep in the Toutle River Valley. This all occurred on March 19th, 1982.[73] Put differently, this canyon system was formed in a single day. Without knowing this important fact, evolutionists would assume it took an enormous amount of time for a river or some other natural source to slowly carve it out. Certainly, this is how evolutionists believe the Grand Canyon was formed.

Supposedly, a little bit of water over an extremely long period of time carved out the Grand Canyon. People who believe in the biblical account of creation disagree. The Bible, a reliable, eyewitness account of world history, records that a catastrophic global flood[74] occurred which involved a great deal of volcanic and seismic activity.[75] While Mount Saint Helens was a local event that caused major damage, including the rapid erosion of a canyon system, the global flood described in the Bible caused catastrophic damage worldwide. Instead of a little bit of water over a long period of time, Christians believe the Grand Canyon was carved out by a lot of water over a little period of time. This belief is consistent with observed rapid canyon formation, but the system in the Toutle River Valley is hardly the only example. Providence Canyon in Georgia was formed rapidly[76] and Burlingame Canyon, in the great state of Washington like the Toutle River Valley, was carved out in about a week.[77] Since we've seen canyons form in a short amount of time, why not assume the same for canyons whose formation hasn't been observed? On top of that, we've never seen a canyon form slowly with just a little bit of water, so why would we assume this happened with canyons whose formation hasn't been observed? It may be popular, but this assumption just doesn't hold water, much like the belief that dinosaurs went extinct about 65 million years ago.

After all, if dinosaurs were really 65 million years old, why have scientists found dinosaur bones with red blood cells, blood vessels and soft tissue? Dr. Mary Schweitzer, one of the researchers who discovered dinosaur bones with red blood cells, pointed out "If you take a blood sample, and you stick it on a shelf, you have nothing recognizable in about a week. So why would there be anything left in dinosaurs?"[78] Bones that are millions of years old couldn't possibly have red blood cells, blood vessels and soft tissue in them. The only explanation, of course, is that dinosaurs haven't been extinct for 65 million years.

On the contrary, God created everything in six days, approximately 6,000 years ago. This obviously included dinosaurs. Now, you might be asking "Does the Bible even talk about dinosaurs?" Well, the word 'dinosaur' wasn't invented until 1841 by Sir Richard Owen. Since the Bible was translated into English in the 16th and 17th centuries, it makes sense the word dinosaur isn't in English translations of the Bible. This doesn't mean the Bible doesn't talk about dinosaurs. In fact, the Bible gives a very detailed description of an animal that sounds a lot like a Brachiosaurus or a Diplodocus. In Job 40, an animal called "behemoth" is described as eating "grass like an ox" while having bones "like bars of iron" and a "tail like a cedar."[79] Some have claimed this "behemoth" was a hippo or an elephant, although both animals have tails that bear a closer resemblance to twigs than cedar trees. Clearly, no animal alive today fits such a description.

Still, if dinosaurs really lived with humans, we would expect to find a lot of historical records of their existence. This is exactly what we find. There are numerous references from the past about creatures we would today call dinosaurs. These creatures are called dragons. The earliest English translations of the Bible, published around 400 years ago, use the word dragon numerous times.[80] The Bible, however, is hardly the only reference to dragons throughout history.

For example, the Chinese lunar calendar uses 12 animals to mark years. Some of these animals include the dog, the tiger and the horse, among others. One of these animals is a dragon. Now, why would the calendar have 11 real animals, and one imaginary animal? China is also known for their artwork, especially pottery, with dragons on it. The country even had a national flag, replaced in 1911, with a dragon emblem. Incidentally, the flag of Wales has the image of a dragon on it to this day. To the north of Wales, there are some interesting brass engravings in Carlisle Cathedral of England. Made late in the 15th century, these engravings depict creatures that look remarkably similar to long-necked sauropod dinosaurs, like a Brachiosaurus. How could people in the 15th century know what a dinosaur looked like, unless they had seen them? Yet, these engravings are far from the only representation of dinosaur-like creatures in artwork over the years.

In addition, stories of heroic dragon-slayers are quite common throughout history, with Beowulf and St. George being the most well-known accounts. Surely, dinosaurs would've been a serious threat to human well-being, so they would've been hunted down. This task wouldn't have been easy, which is why a successful dragon-slayer earned so much attention. This likely had a great deal to do with the disappearance of dinosaurs. Many animals have gone extinct. Often, human beings have played a direct role. On top of being hunted, dinosaur's habitats would've also been compromised by growing human settlement. As a result, we don't run into T-Rex's today. Still, the historical references are consistent with dinosaurs having lived alongside human beings. For those skeptical of accounts from the past, the discovery of 'fresh' dinosaur bones with red blood cells in them is difficult to dismiss. What's more, these dinosaur bones aren't the only scientific observation consistent with a young earth.[81]

First off, many other fossils assumed to be millions of years old have been found with DNA in them.[82] DNA is maintained by repair mechanisms in living cells. After death, with these repair mechanisms gone, DNA begins to decay rapidly. In other words, DNA can't last in natural environments for millions of years.[83] So, how could fossils thought to be millions of years old have DNA in them? Speaking of DNA, the genetic information in the human population has been steadily breaking down over the years because of mutations.[84] This is known as genetic entropy. Every generation, more genetic defects accumulate in the human population. As more mutations accumulate, there is less usable genetic information because more genes have been corrupted. So, if humans have existed for hundreds of thousands of years, we should be near extinction or extinct already. Still, genetic information isn't all that has been observed to be decaying.

According to measurements, the strength of the earth's magnetic field is rapidly decreasing.[85] The earth's magnetic field is caused by a decaying electric current in the earth's core. If this electric current was billions of years old, at current decay rates, its strength in the past would've been so large that the earth would've broken apart and melted. Even if we assume the decay rates aren't constant, measured decay rates are consistent with a young earth. Comets, assumed to be billions of years old like the earth, would've also disappeared if they were really that old.[86] When these mixtures of ice, dust and other particles pass by the sun, they lose a great deal of their mass. They couldn't possibly last for billions of years. While scientific observation points to a young age for comets, evolutionists have made several unlikely and unobserved assumptions to explain why they are still around. Since the age of the earth is a very important element of their belief in evolution, they will make any assumptions necessary to defend the faith.

A Choice of Miracles

We all believe in miracles. Everyone has a choice between two miraculous accounts of how we all got here. Evolution is the belief nature created itself in direct violation of numerous scientific laws. The biblical account of creation is the belief one eternal, all-powerful God supernaturally created the universe. Which miracle is more believable? Which miraculous account is consistent with the world around us?

Let's say you believe in evolution. You believe nothing created matter, in spite of the First Law of Thermodynamics. This matter made itself expand, despite the Law of Inertia. Next, non-living chemicals created a living organism, violating the Law of Biogenesis. This living organism also had DNA, but as yet, no natural mechanism has been found to explain where DNA originally came from. Then, natural selection is believed to have made this living organism more complex, although the selection process reduces genetic information over time. These beliefs can't be explained by natural laws or observed processes, so they are supernatural explanations. These miracles are accepted by faith. How do you know these miracles happened? No one was there to see them. Since you can't be sure, what if you're wrong?

On the other hand, believing in the biblical account of creation requires only one assumption: God is who He says He is. In other words, God is eternal and all-powerful, so supernaturally creating the universe is no big deal. Where did matter come from? God created it with space and time. Where did life come from? The living God gave life. Where did genetic information come from? God designed the complex information storage system known as DNA. How do Christians know? Well, the Bible is the written Word of God. It is a reliable eyewitness account of how we all got here. In the beginning, God created the Heavens and the earth, and it was all perfect. Obviously, that's not how we find things today. The written Word of God tells us why.

Corruption

In every way, Adam and Eve had the good life, but this didn't last long. God told them they could eat from any tree in the Garden of Eden, except the one called the Tree of the Knowledge of Good and Evil.[87] If they disobeyed, they would immediately die spiritually, being separated from God. They would also begin to die physically from that day forward. Well, they chose to disobey. Satan, who had rebelled against God shortly after the week of creation, had taken the form of a snake.[88] He knew God told Adam and Eve not to eat the fruit of a certain tree, so he tempted Eve by questioning God's command.[89] He then lied to Eve, saying that if she ate of the tree she wouldn't die.[90] Instead, he told her she would be like God, "knowing good and evil."[91] Eve liked the sound of deciding what was right and wrong for herself. She quickly ate the fruit of the tree and gave some to Adam, who freely ate it. He also wanted to live by his own rules. Adam and Eve wanted to be God.

It didn't work out like they hoped. Their disobedience was sin, or rebellion, against God. Like their tempter Satan, they had rebelled against the authority of their Creator. Since God is perfectly just, He had to punish Adam and Eve's sin. He cursed His creation as the righteous punishment for their sin. They wanted life without God, and so God gave them a glimpse of what life without Him is like. Known as 'the Fall,' Adam and Eve's sin brought pain, suffering and death into the world.[92] Their sin corrupted all of creation. Thorns, disease, decay and death were now facts of life. The corrupted creation, with evils like disease and death, was hardly the only consequence of sin. Indeed, all of Adam's descendants would inherit his sinful nature.

All of us are separated from God at birth. If you're a parent, you know this all too well. After all, children don't need anyone to teach them how to do the wrong thing. Naturally, since God gave us free will and we're all born with a sinful nature, evil is everywhere. It has nothing to do with a bad childhood or a rough environment, everybody falls short of God's perfect standard.[93] We're all guilty of sin, and our sinful choices promote suffering. The corrupted creation and the corrupted human race are the sources of all the evil in the world. This corruption is entirely the result of human sin. It is the punishment for wanting to be God, personally deciding what's good and evil, and all of us are born with this same desire.

But, it's not all doom and gloom. God didn't abandon His creation after sin entered the world. He promised to provide a way for us to escape the ultimate consequence of sin: eternal separation from Him. At the appointed time, He would send a Savior to crush the head of the snake.[94] In other words, this Savior would deliver us from our sins, dealing a knockout blow to Satan. Still, due to Adam and Eve's rebellion, everyone was now born under the power of sin. Their first son, Cain, behaved accordingly. In a jealous rage, he murdered his younger brother Abel. He was forced to wander the earth as punishment, and soon he and his wife began having children of their own.[95]

At this point, people who have faith in evolution usually ask, "Who was Cain's wife?" Well, the Bible says Adam and Eve had many other sons and daughters whose names aren't recorded in the text.[96] So, Cain married one of his sisters. Often, evolutionists are outraged by this. Of course, if evolution is true, they have no reason to be outraged over anything. If there is no God, there is no absolute moral code. Anything goes. What's right and wrong is decided by human opinion, so brother-sister marriage couldn't possibly be definitively 'wrong.' By whose standard would it be 'bad?' How could an evolutionist be so judgmental, forcing their opinion of right and wrong on others?

Typically, they'll respond by saying "Doesn't the Bible forbid brother-sister marriage? Why would Cain be allowed to marry his sister then?" Certainly, the Bible forbids brother-sister marriage, but God didn't give this law until the time of Moses.[97] When brothers and sisters married each other before the time of Moses, they weren't breaking God's law. Why did God wait until the time of Moses to outlaw marriage between close relatives? These days, brothers and sisters aren't legally allowed to marry and have children. This is because the children of a brother-sister union have a much higher probability of being born with deformities.

All children inherit one set of genes from their mother and another set from their father. Unfortunately, genes today contain many mistakes because of the corruption of creation, the result of Adam and Eve's sin. The closer two people are related to one another, the more likely it is they will have similar mutations in their genes. This is because they have inherited genes from the same parents. If a brother and sister married and had children, their kids would inherit similar sets of genes from each of them. Since the genes have similar mutations, they will pair together and create deformities in the children.

So, why did God wait until the time of Moses? Simply put, Adam and Eve didn't have any genetic mutations. After their sin corrupted creation, disease, decay and death became facts of life. Every generation, more mistakes accumulate in all living organisms. While mutations crept into the human population over time, they wouldn't have been significant early on. Cain, and his brothers and sisters, would've had relatively few genetic mutations because Adam and Eve had perfect genes. There would've been no threat of a brother and sister having children with deformities. By the time of Moses, however, the situation was much different. Roughly 2,500 years after Adam and Eve's sin, a dangerous amount of genetic mutations had accumulated in the human population. It was necessary for God to make marriage between close relatives illegal. Besides, there were also plenty of people on the earth by this time. Close relatives didn't need to be marrying anymore.

Of course, since genetic mistakes accumulate every generation, this presents a problem for evolutionists. If evolution is true, why would brother-sister marriage be a genetic problem? Why would mutations be increasing over time? How did a one-celled organism ever gain the usable information to turn into a human over billions of years? Over time, there would be less usable information in this organism's population due to genetic mutations. Surely, if any organism had been alive for hundreds of thousands of years, that organism would be extinct or near extinction today.

At this, people who believe in evolution usually ask "How can you really believe all humans came from one man and one woman?" This is an odd question, considering evolutionists believe all humans came from a one-celled organism, which came from non-living chemicals in spite of scientific law. Regardless, the Bible records many of Cain's descendants took after him. They had all inherited Adam's sinful nature. The world was filled with evil, and God had to administer justice on a global scale.

Catastrophe

Following in the footsteps of their ancestors, the descendants of Adam and Eve turned their backs on their Creator. They lived by their own rules, and evil was all over the place. The wickedness of the human race was so great, only Noah trusted in God.[98] God decided to judge the world by sending a global flood, but because of Noah's faith, God saved him and his family. He instructed Noah to build the Ark.[99] When the Ark was complete, God brought pairs of every air-breathing land animal and bird to board the Ark, along with seven pairs of a few animals.[100]

Now, you're probably wondering, "How did all of the animals fit?"[101] For starters, Noah only took air-breathing and land-dwelling animals on the Ark.[102] He didn't have to round all of these creatures up. God brought them to the Ark.[103] He also didn't have to take all the species of animals we see today, just the original kinds God created. Only two dogs would've been on board, not two poodles, two wolves and two coyotes. Given the large amount of genetic information these original kinds had, only two dogs were needed to give rise to all of the dog species we see today. Naturally, the animals on the Ark were younger. Younger animals would be around a lot longer after the Flood to repopulate the earth, and they also took up less space. Of course, the Ark didn't have to carry sea creatures because they wouldn't have faced extinction from a global flood. Likewise, there was no need to take plants. They could've survived as seeds or on floating mats of vegetation. Insects could've also survived on these mats and on other debris. That said, if insects were on the Ark, they take up very little space.

Not that space was a problem on the Ark. It was an enormous ship. The Ark was approximately 450 feet long, 75 feet wide and 44 feet high.[104] There was plenty of room for Noah, his family, the animals and all of the provisions for the trip. But, you might ask, "How did Noah and his family care for all of the animals on board?" Well, these animals were in cages of some sort, as God commanded Noah to build "rooms" on the Ark.[105] He also told Noah to take food for his family and the animals.[106] So, the Ark probably had dried food. It's likely there were grains on board to feed the animals, and for the carnivores, they could've brought salted meat. Also, troughs could've been near the animal's cages to reduce the amount of work Noah and his family had to do. Noah probably packed some drinking water on board, but rainwater certainly could've been collected from outside. If it was, it could've been piped directly into troughs, though there was plenty of room to store food and water. Noah and his family likely didn't have to spend a lot of time dealing with animal waste either. They could've built sloped floors where waste would've fallen outside of the Ark, or raised cages with slatted floors. They could've also brought sawdust or other absorbents along for the ride. In addition, since the animals on board were younger, their space, food and waste requirements definitely wouldn't have been as great as some people might initially think. This includes the various dinosaur kinds.

While some dinosaurs grew to be very large, most of them didn't. Massive dinosaurs also weren't born that big, as even the biggest dinosaur eggs are less than 2 feet long. In addition, the dinosaurs on the Ark didn't grow too big during their stay. Growth studies of dinosaur bones show that dinosaurs had a teenage growth spurt.[107] They were only on the Ark for a little over a year,[108] so their growth spurt wouldn't have been a concern. When it was time to leave the Ark, these younger dinosaurs managed to fit through the door just fine.

At this point, you may be thinking "How could Noah build such a huge ship?" Well, Noah didn't build it by himself. The massive Ark took roughly 70 years for Noah and his sons to complete.[109] He could've also used hired hands. Still, Noah and his family were more than capable. They were at least as smart and strong as people today, and quite likely, they were stronger and smarter. After all, they were a lot closer to the perfect genetic code of Adam than we are. Regardless, building the Ark wouldn't have been a problem.

With Noah, his family, and all the animals on board, the "fountains of the great deep" broke open and the "windows of heaven" opened up.[110] The breaking open of the "fountains of the great deep" provided most of the floodwaters. Worldwide, the earth's crust fractured and water shot up out of the ground. There were violent earthquakes, volcanic activity, and hot water gushing out of the earth. To this day, there is a lot of water stored below ground.[111] Before the "fountains of the great deep" broke open, there was significantly more water beneath the earth's surface. We know God formed the earth out of water, and on the third day of creation, made dry land appear.[112] Certain portions of the sea-floor sank down and water drained off the land, trapping water underneath the land. During the Flood, gushing water from beneath the earth's surface covered the earth from below, while driving rain falling from the "windows of heaven" covered the earth from above.

Where did all of this water go? Due to geological activity during the Flood, mountain ranges were uplifted and ocean basins were formed. The floodwaters settled in these ocean basins. Currently, about 70% of the earth is covered by water. Indeed, if the surface of the earth was leveled out, it would be completely covered by water. Additionally, the waters from the Flood are largely responsible for the billions of dead things we find buried in rock layers around the globe. After all, when an animal dies, it decays and is picked apart by scavengers. In other words, the animal's carcass isn't preserved. No fossilization can occur. With the Flood, however, living animals were rapidly buried by water, sand and mud. As a result, we find billions of well-preserved fossils all over the earth. Now, some people may ask, "If there was a global flood, why don't we find more human fossils?"

Simply put, most people wouldn't have been rapidly buried by water, sand and mud. As the waters rose, they would've headed for higher ground. They would've held on to logs and other floating debris. Naturally, when they died, their bodies would've been left to decompose. Only Noah and his family lived to tell the tale, and they definitely passed it on to their descendants. While the details vary, likely because of centuries of retelling, remote cultures all over the world have a record of a catastrophic global flood. Flood legends from ancient cultures in India, China, Greece, Hawaii, Russia, Italy, Australia, Perú and México, among others, share many similarities with the global Flood recorded in Genesis.[113]

In addition to worldwide flood legends and billions of well-preserved fossils, the Flood also gave rise to a lengthy ice age. Many evolutionists believe there were multiple ice ages, but they aren't sure how any of them came about. The problem is simple. To have a large amount of ice form on land, there needs to be a lot of snowfall. Snow requires evaporation, and evaporation requires heat. Having a cold climate won't produce a lot of ice, because the colder the weather is the less evaporation there will be. This means less snow. In other words, the only way to have an ice age is to have a cold climate and lots of evaporation at the same time. What could cause such a scenario?

People who believe in the biblical account of creation maintain there was one Ice Age, and it was a result of the global Flood. When "the fountains of the great deep" broke open, a lot of hot water gushed out. This water eventually settled in deep ocean basins, formed during the Flood. The water, being warm, would've led to a lot of evaporation. All the while, there would've been volcanic eruptions. The ash from these eruptions would've been in the air. This would block out a lot of sunlight, causing landmasses to cool. So, the warm oceans produced evaporation, which led to snowfall over continents cooled by volcanic ash blocking sunlight. Snow would've piled up and ice sheets would've formed. After a few centuries, the oceans would've cooled down. There would be less evaporation and less snowfall. Likewise, volcanic ash would've disappeared. Sunlight would've poured in and gradually melted snow and ice, ending the Ice Age.[114]

Still, some people might wonder, "Did the Flood really have to be global?" Well, if the Flood was local, why would Noah have to build the Ark? He could've taken the animals and headed to an area where the floodwaters wouldn't reach them. Also, why would birds have been sent on board? They could have flown to higher ground without any problem. Most importantly, God sent the Flood to judge the wickedness of everybody on the earth. Noah alone trusted in God. Due to his faith, he and his family were the only people on earth that were saved. God provided a way of salvation for Noah and his family, but the Ark had plenty of room for additional passengers.

While Noah was faithfully building the Ark, many people saw his progress. It's quite likely Noah was asked about his construction project, and when he answered, most people probably made fun of him. Surely, many people of that time were too absorbed with their lives to even care. Yet, the Bible describes Noah as a "preacher of righteousness."[115] Quite possibly, Noah warned people passing by that a global flood was on its way. For several decades, the people of Noah's day had a choice. They could keep doing what was right in their own eyes, rebelling against their Creator, or they could trust in God by walking through the door of the Ark. Despite their corrupt ways, God provided a way of salvation. They refused His mercy. When the door of the Ark was shut, their rebellion was judged. Sadly, many of Noah's descendants also chose to rebel against their Creator. Judgment ensued.

Confusion

After the Flood, God commanded Noah and his family to spread out and fill the earth.[116] Noah's descendants disobeyed. They chose to stay in one place, building a tall tower not only to glorify themselves, but also to worship the stars.[117] Instead of obeying God's command, they tried to replace Him. They wanted to be God, deciding what was right and wrong for themselves. For guidance in their daily lives, they looked to the planets and the stars. They worshipped the creation rather than the Creator.

Their rebellion didn't work out like they planned. At that time, everyone spoke the same language. To punish the disobedience of Noah's descendants, God confused their language so they couldn't understand each other. By confusing their language, God scattered them all over the earth. These days, we have thousands of languages, but researchers suggest there are approximately just 136 language families.[118] The original language families were created at the Tower of Babel, and they gradually branched out into the large number of languages we have today.

On the other hand, evolutionists aren't sure where all of the world's languages came from. Atheist Richard Dawkins admitted "I am biased towards thinking it was gradual, but it is not quite obvious that it had to be. Some people think it began suddenly, more or less invented by a single genius in a particular place at a particular time."[119] Although Dr. Dawkins admits the possibility that a 'single genius' could've invented human language, he rejects the possibility this could've been God. That said, most people who believe in evolution think all the languages of the world originally came from animal grunts. This hasn't been observed, so they accept this belief by faith. Grunting is assumed to have given rise to simple human speech, which supposedly produced more sophisticated languages over time. As yet, no mechanism has been suggested to explain any of this. In addition, there is no pattern of simpler languages becoming more sophisticated. Ancient languages are anything but simple. If they were, speaking classical Greek would be a breeze. Besides, modern English speakers have enough trouble reading Shakespeare, as any high school English student will tell you.

Regardless, God's punishment of Noah's descendants at the Tower of Babel did more than disrupt their construction project. The workers were instantly unable to communicate with anyone outside of their extended family group. The language barriers between different groups meant they wouldn't be able to relate to one another. Quite likely, there was hostility between these groups. So, they moved away from each other, spreading out over the earth as God had commanded. With this in mind, you might be wondering, "If we're all descended from Adam and Eve, where did all of the different races come from?"

For starters, there is only one human race. No matter what skin color two people may have, they can have intercourse and produce perfectly healthy children. In fact, the genetic differences of any two people from around the globe are usually only 0.2%.[120] According to genetic studies, different 'races' don't exist, confirming the Bible's claim that we are all one human family.[121] Yet, if we're all related, why do we look so different from one another? Well, Noah's descendants had a lot of genetic variety. After the confusion at Babel, they split up and spread out over the earth. These smaller groups had different amounts of genetic information for various characteristics. One of these physical features was skin color.

Everybody produces melanin, a brown coloring pigment in the skin. Melanin protects the skin from damage done by the sun's rays. The amount of melanin we produce is controlled by our genes. People with a lot of melanin have dark skin, while individuals with little melanin have light skin. Before the confusion at Babel, there was one large population that spoke the same language. Within this large group, there was a lot of genetic variety. The population would've had genes for dark and light skin, so most people would've had brown skin. Since there weren't any cultural or language barriers keeping people from marrying each other, the average skin color wouldn't have changed much. After Babel, with the population split up, smaller groups with less genetic variety spread out over the earth. Some groups had more genes for darker skin, while other groups had more genes for lighter skin. When these groups moved, people with genes for lighter skin would survive in environments with less sun, and people with genes for darker skin would survive in sunny environments.

Naturally, some groups of people died out, because they didn't have the genetic information to adjust to their surroundings. The Neanderthals of Europe, for example, appear to have suffered from rickets. Rickets, a vitamin D deficiency, is a potentially fatal disease that causes severe bone deformities. When the body is exposed to sunlight, it produces vitamin D. The darker the skin, the less vitamin D it produces. So, Neanderthals were likely dark-skinned people who had genes that weren't suited for their new, less sunny environment.

In addition to having different amounts of genetic information, the various people groups also took with them different skills. Some groups knew more about farming, while others knew more about building or making metal tools. Other groups didn't know much about farming, engineering or technology. They would've had to learn these skills on their own by trial and error. Since they had little knowledge of building or metal-working, they would've found existing shelters and made use of the most durable material around for tools. So, they lived in caves and used stone tools, at least until they were able to build settlements and make metal tools. The Ice Age caused by the Flood would've also made people more likely to seek shelter from the cold as quickly as possible. Cave shelters would've been attractive for groups moving north. Clearly, people groups after Babel found it convenient to live in caves and use stone tools for various reasons.

Contrary to popular belief, there was never a 'stone age' with sub-human 'cavemen.' Sadly, this view of history has done a great deal of harm. Indeed, if evolution is true, the different people groups around the world 'evolved' separately over many thousands of years. This belief has given rise to the idea that some 'races' are more superior to other 'races.' Adolph Hitler wasn't the only evolutionist to think so. Even evolutionist, atheist and anti-racist Stephen Jay Gould admitted, "Biological arguments for racism may have been common before 1850, but they increased by orders of magnitude following the acceptance of evolutionary theory."[122] Despite the teaching of evolution, however, there are no 'races.' We are all one human family, and unfortunately, we all share the same sinful nature. The revolt at the Tower of Babel, the rebellion before the Flood and the rejection in the Garden of Eden show we all have a serious problem with sin. Thankfully, God did something about it once and for all.

Christ

The history of the human race isn't pretty. Like the first man and woman, we have all lived by our own set of rules. To make matters worse, no one can earn God's forgiveness by doing good deeds, because nothing we do can erase our wrongdoing.[123] Fortunately, God has provided a way to be saved from judgment. The Father sent His Son, Jesus, on a rescue mission. The Lord Jesus added a human nature to His divine nature, so He could save us from our sins. But, you may ask, "If there is only one God, how can Jesus be God?"

In the beginning, God spoke the universe into existence. When it came time to make man, "God said, Let us make man in our image, after our likeness."[124] This wasn't a grammatical mistake. In fact, Jesus Himself spoke these very words. In the Book of John, we are told "In the beginning was the Word, and the Word was with God, and the Word was God."[125] Jesus is the Word, who is God and was with God in the beginning. Indeed, "All things were made by him,"[126] and "by him all things consist."[127] Jesus Christ, the eternal, almighty Word, created the universe by His word. Before He spoke light into being, "the earth was without form" and the "Spirit of God moved upon the face of the waters."[128] The Father laid out the plan for creation, the Son spoke the creation into existence and the Holy Spirit energized it.

At the baptism of Jesus, the Holy Spirit was seen descending like a dove and landing upon the Son, with the voice of the Father heard from Heaven saying "This is my beloved Son, in whom I am well pleased."[129] After His death and Resurrection, Jesus commanded His followers to baptize "in the name of the Father, and of the Son, and of the Holy Ghost."[130] He said 'the name of,' not names, because the Father, the Son and the Holy Spirit have the same name: God. The one God of the universe exists in three distinct, co-equal Persons: Father, Son, and Holy Spirit. There isn't one person and three persons, or one god and three gods. God is three-in-one. He is one in essence and three in Person, so there is no contradiction.

Understanding this can be challenging, and while no illustration is perfect, the triune nature of God can be compared to the sun. The Father is like the sun, the Son is like the light coming from the sun and the Holy Spirit is like the heat of the sun. The sun is the source of the light. Without the sun, there would be no light. Of course, it's impossible to have the sun without light and heat. Without light, the sun would be invisible. We couldn't see the sun without its bright light. Without heat, we can't feel the warmth of the sun's rays. We wouldn't know the warmth of the sun without its heat. The sun has always emitted light and heat. So, the light and heat that come from the sun are equal to the sun. Jesus is the "light of the world"[131] and "the image of the invisible God."[132] The Son added a human nature to His divine nature so that by Him we might see the fullness of God.[133] The Creator became a part of His creation, showing the world the "light of the knowledge of the glory of God in the face of Jesus Christ."[134]

Only God can save.[135] When a jailer asked imprisoned Christians how he could be saved, he was told to "Believe on the Lord Jesus Christ, and thou shalt be saved."[136] The jailer trusted in Jesus Christ, went home and "rejoiced, believing in God."[137] Believing in Jesus Christ and believing in God are one and the same, for Jesus is "the great God and our Saviour."[138] Only God can be worshipped.[139]At seeing the risen Jesus, a follower of Jesus named Thomas fell before Him and worshipfully proclaimed "My LORD and my God."[140] Only God is without sin. The Lord Jesus lived a life "without sin."[141] To save us from our sins, so that we might be able to love and worship Him, His perfect life would have to end in a sacrificial death.

Cross

Let's say you broke the law. You have to pay a fine, but you don't have enough money to do so. You might tell the judge it won't happen again, but you still have to pay the fine. You may say you're sorry, but the punishment still stands. You could even bring up all of the good deeds you've ever done, but that won't erase the crime you've committed. Justice must be served. You have to pay the penalty, unless someone pays it for you.

Since we have all lived by our own rules, we have all rejected God's authority.

Doing a lot of good deeds can't take away the crimes we've committed. Justice must be served. We must be punished for our sins, unless someone perfect suffers the punishment in our place. Someone did. Jesus said "For God so loved the world, that he gave his only begotten Son, that whosoever believeth in him should not perish, but have everlasting life."[142] Jesus, the Son of God, added a human nature to His divine nature to pay the penalty for our sins. He had to add a human nature so He could suffer our punishment for us. The punishment for rejecting God's authority is severe. After all, the punishment must fit the crime. Yet, our Creator became a part of His creation to die in our place. Our Creator became our Savior.

Of course, Jesus couldn't be defeated by death. After He was crucified, Jesus was buried in the tomb of a wealthy gentleman named Joseph of Arimathea.[143] This fulfilled a prophecy made many hundreds of years earlier.[144] Now, since Jesus predicted He would rise again three days after His death,[145] the Jewish and Roman authorities made sure His followers wouldn't steal His body.[146] The tomb of the Lord Jesus was guarded by several armed men, and they sealed the heavy stone door of the tomb tightly shut.[147] Three days later, Jesus rose from the dead, showing His power over all things.[148] The tomb was empty,[149] just as He had predicted. Over the years, this fact has troubled people who reject the Resurrection. How could a guarded tomb that was sealed by an extremely heavy stone be empty? To add to their discomfort, Jesus appeared to several people after He rose again over a period of 40 days,[150] including more than 500 people at one time.[151] In an effort to dismiss the Resurrection, they've let their imaginations run wild.

For example, some people have suggested everyone got confused and went to the wrong tomb. Frankly, this requires more faith than believing in the Resurrection. First off, did Joseph of Arimathea suddenly forget where his own tomb was located? In addition, did all of the guards forget which tomb they were supposed to be keeping an eye on? When everybody came to their senses and realized their collective memory lapses, why didn't anyone bother to find the right tomb? Surely, the Jewish leaders and Roman authorities would've done so. Why didn't they head on over to the correct tomb and assure everyone the body of Jesus was still there? Besides, 'mass confusion' doesn't account for Jesus' physical appearances to a bunch of different people over a period of 40 days. As a result, many individuals think the followers of Jesus must've experienced a series of hallucinations too.

The Bible says Jesus appeared to different groups of people on multiple occasions,[152] including an appearance to more than 500 people at one time.[153] So, according to this belief, several groups of people had shared hallucinations in different places and at different times. This would be a miracle in its own right. On top of that, Jesus' appearances were clearly physical. On one occasion, a group of His followers initially thought they were seeing a ghost.[154] Jesus responded by showing them His hands and feet, complete with nail marks, and He invited them to touch Him.[155] After this, He ate some broiled fish and taught them awhile.[156] In other words, Jesus was really with them, in a real, physical body. If Jesus' disciples were hallucinating, however, why didn't the Jewish leaders and Roman authorities show everybody the body of Jesus? Apparently, everyone 'hallucinated' the empty tomb also.

To get around this stumbling block, some people have put forth the idea that Jesus never really died. Instead, they believe He passed out and woke up three days later. Let's put this in perspective. Jesus' suffering began the night of His arrest in the Garden of Gethsemane. While He prayed to the Father, He was in such agony that His sweat fell like "great drops of blood."[157] This rare condition is known as hematidrosis. After His arrest, Jesus was beaten by some of the Jewish leaders.[158] From there, He was scourged by Roman soldiers.[159] Jesus was bound to a post and whipped repeatedly. Next, some Roman soldiers made a crown of thorns and put it on His head.[160] They struck Him on the head with a staff, which drove the thorns into His scalp.[161] At this point, it's amazing Jesus was even conscious. Finally, He was crucified. By definition, this would've been excruciating, a term which literally means 'out of crucifying.' Since crucifixion was a painfully slow death, victims would sometimes have their legs broken to speed up the inevitable. The Jewish leaders requested that this be done to Jesus.[162] The Roman soldiers broke the legs of the two criminals crucified along with Jesus,[163] but when they came to Him, they "saw that he was dead already" and didn't break His legs.[164]

Incidentally, this fulfilled a prophecy made hundreds of years earlier which predicted none of Jesus' bones would be broken.[165] Instead of breaking His legs, one of the soldiers pierced Jesus' side with a spear to verify He was dead.[166] This clinched the diagnosis of death by crucifixion. Could the Roman soldiers have made a mistake?

Considering their job description required executing people, it's highly doubtful they were too incompetent to figure out if Jesus was really dead. Still, even if Jesus somehow managed to survive being scourged, crucified and having His side pierced with a spear, how did He survive three days in a cold tomb without food and water? How did He have the strength to roll back the heavy, sealed stone door of the tomb He was buried in? Likewise, He would've needed serious medical attention, including a visit to the emergency room, heavy-grade antibiotics and a tetanus shot. Given the poor state of His health, why were all of His disciples convinced He had conquered death when they saw Him?

Simply put, everyone accepted Jesus' death and burial. Even His enemies did. His enemies also never challenged the fact that His tomb was empty three days later. On the contrary, to explain why He wasn't there, they made up the story that His followers stole the body.[167] They bribed the guards to say "His disciples came by night, and stole him away while we slept."[168] How did the sleeping guards know who stole the body if their eyes were shut? It's tough to say. It's also very hard to believe Jesus' disciples overpowered a group of armed guards and removed a massive, tightly-sealed boulder to take His body, especially since they were hiding in fear after His death.[169] Why would they have wanted to steal His body anyway? Although Jesus told them to expect His Resurrection, the Bible says His disciples didn't understand He was going to rise from the grave.[170] After Jesus was crucified, they were mourning His loss, not eagerly awaiting His Resurrection.[171] Additionally, why would a group of frightened disciples suddenly turn into courageous preachers by stealing His body?[172] Why would they risk their lives for a lie?

For instance, just before Jesus was crucified, a disciple named Peter denied he knew Him three times.[173] After Jesus rose again, Peter proclaimed the Resurrection boldly,[174] even in front of some of the Jewish leaders who had condemned Jesus to death.[175] Stephen, a young follower of Jesus, delivered an uncompromising message to this very group of Jewish leaders.[176] He was promptly stoned to death.[177] One gentleman in attendance was Saul of Tarsus, more commonly known as the Apostle Paul.[178] He was a ruthless persecutor of Christians,[179] until Jesus appeared to Him.[180] He immediately became a Christian. Thomas, another follower of Jesus, also wasn't convinced until Jesus appeared to him. He said that unless "I shall see in his hands the print of the nails, and put my finger into the print of the nails, and thrust my hand into his side, I will not believe."[181] When Jesus appeared to Thomas, He told him to look at His hands, put his finger in the nail marks and thrust his hand into His side.[182] Thomas worshipfully responded "My LORD and my God."[183] The same followers with fears and doubts soon risked their lives to proclaim the Resurrection of Jesus Christ, the guarantee that our sins had been fully paid for.[184] The death of the Lord Jesus paid for our sins; His Resurrection was the receipt saying "paid in full." The Father accepted the sacrificial death of the Son, so our case before Him can legally be dismissed. One day, Jesus will return. All things will be restored, and He will rule forever and ever.

Consummation

In the beginning, God created a world without pain, suffering and death. Everything was perfect. Yet, this came to an abrupt end when

Adam and Eve rejected God's authority. They wanted life without God, so their punishment fit the crime. God gave them a glimpse of what life without Him is like. Disease, pain, suffering and death entered the world through the rebellion of the first human beings. Since all of us have inherited Adam's sinful nature, all of us have sinned. We have all lived by our own set of rules; we have all told God we don't need Him. As a result, evil is everywhere. Thankfully, this will not always be the case.

Contrary to popular belief, Christians won't be floating around on clouds and playing harps for eternity. In the future, God is going to make "a new heaven and a new earth."[185] He will restore His creation. There will be no pain, sickness, suffering and death.[186] Sin and evil will no longer exist. The creation will be as it was meant to be, for everything will be perfect. But, people who don't believe in God often say "This sounds too good to be true. Why would God allow so much evil in the first place? Why do bad things happen to good people?"

First off, people who reject God's existence have no basis to ask these questions. After all, if there is no God, there is no absolute authority. So, 'good' and 'evil' are simply matters of personal preference. Saying "rape is wrong" would be no different than saying "I like chocolate ice cream more than vanilla ice cream." While most people think rape is evil, rapists don't have a problem with it. Whose opinion is right? Hitler murdered millions of people trying to create a 'master race,' all in the name of speeding up the 'evolutionary process.' Most Germans agreed with him at the time. Was what Nazi Germany did evil? Most people who reject God say it was, but on what grounds? If God doesn't exist, what's 'good' and 'evil' would be decided by personal opinion. It would make no sense to accuse anyone of being 'good' or 'bad.' They simply have different preferences. Why would one person's preferences be more or less 'evil' or 'good' than the preferences of another person?

Of course, only God determines what is good and evil. According to His standard of right and wrong, human beings definitely don't fall into the good category. In other words, there are no "good people." Why doesn't God stop evil? Well, God has given everybody free will. Since everyone is born with a sinful nature, it's not a surprise evil is all over the place. To put it another way, if God decided to rid the world of evil, none of us would be here. Yet, God does more than just put up with the evil of sin.

The corrupted creation, with disease, death and other evils, was the righteous punishment for the sin of Adam and Eve. They wanted life without God, so God gave them a glimpse of what life without Him is like. Still, this punishment served a loving purpose. We have all lived by our own rules. We've all told God we don't need Him in our lives, so the ultimate punishment for sin is complete separation from our Creator for eternity. To avoid this eternal punishment, God allows pain and suffering in our lives to get our attention. C.S. Lewis once wrote "God whispers to us in our pleasures, speaks in our conscience, but shouts in our pains. It is his megaphone to rouse a deaf world."[187] Surely, suffering develops compassion, patience and kindness toward others, but God uses evil for a far greater purpose than that.

Evil, whether committed by human hands or the result of the corrupted creation, shows us the horrible nature of sin. Without going through the pain and suffering that sin causes, no one would realize its destructiveness. Nobody would be humbled enough to admit their guilt for committing wrongdoing. Truly, if everything went our way, we'd be spoiled and proud. We wouldn't recognize our need for anyone or anything, but given our sinfulness, we need God to avoid eternal suffering. Pain, suffering and evil of all kinds points us to the greatest act of love of all time: the sacrificial death of Jesus Christ for our sins. Although He never sinned, Jesus was crucified. The height of human evil, however, couldn't overcome the height of God's love. Jesus voluntarily suffered death to pay the penalty for our rebellion against Him. God has a plan to end evil, and the death of Jesus made it possible for us to be a part of the New Earth, where there will be no pain, suffering, disease and death. Everything will be perfect. Over the years, however, several individuals have tried to lead people away from the promise of eternal life. Like the snake cast doubt on what God told Eve in the Garden of Eden,[188] so "wolves" disguised "in sheep's clothing" have attacked the Word of God.[189]

Wolves in Sheep's Clothing

Islam

In recent years, there has been no shortage of headlines about Islam. Naturally, the media coverage and campaign speeches leave a lot to be desired. At its core, Islam is the belief that Allah is the creator of the universe. The Koran is believed to be the perfect revelation of Allah to the world. This revelation was delivered to Muhammad. As a result, the Koran is considered to be superior to the Holy Bible. In fact, many Muslims think the Word of God has been changed and corrupted. While this is a common belief among Muslims, curiously, the Koran frequently states the exact opposite.*

Indeed, the Koran says the Holy Bible is the true revelation of Allah in numerous places.[1] For example, Allah sent down "the Book, confirming what went before it; and He sent down the Law (of Moses) and the Gospel (of Jesus) before this, as a guide to mankind."[2] In addition, Muslims are commanded to say "We believe in Allah, and the revelation given to us, and to Abraham, Isma'il, Isaac, Jacob, and the Tribes, and that given to Moses and Jesus, and that given to (all) prophets from their Lord: We make no difference between one and another of them."[3] According to the Koran, the Bible is the true revelation of Allah, and Muslims are told to believe it. The Koran also says Allah is all-knowing, so "None can change His words."[4] Well, since Allah's words can't be changed and the Bible is said to be Allah's revelation, how could the Holy Bible have been changed and corrupted?

Saying the Holy Bible is corrupt plainly contradicts what the Koran says, but oddly, the Koran itself says its own text has been tampered with. The Koran speaks of the wrath "sent down on those who divided (Scripture into arbitrary parts)"[5] and those individuals who made the Koran "into shreds (as they please)."[6] To put it another way, during the time the Koran was being compiled, people were dividing it up. They were choosing to believe in some parts while rejecting others. Since the text of the Koran was being tampered with during its compilation, how do Muslims know they have the right version of the Koran today? On top of that, the Koran says there are "none that can alter the words (and decrees) of Allah."[7] If no one can change Allah's words and decrees, why were the words of the Koran being changed by various individuals?

Yet, while the Koran says no one can change the words of Allah, it also says "None of Our revelations do We abrogate or cause to be forgotten, but We substitute something better or similar."[8] In other words, later revelations from Allah take the place of earlier revelations from Allah. This doctrine is called abrogation, which is the Muslim belief that whenever there is a discrepancy between two passages, the passage which was revealed later replaces the earlier one. Obviously, this raises several questions. If the words of Allah never change, why would later revelations of Allah be different from Allah's earlier revelations? Why would there be discrepancies between revelations that need to be cancelled out? The Koran claims of itself that "Had it been from other Than Allah, they would surely have found therein Much discrepancy."[9] Since there are discrepancies between earlier and later revelations from Allah recorded in the Koran, does this mean the Koran is "from other Than Allah?" Certainly, people during Muhammad's day must have thought so.

After all, the Koran records "When We substitute one revelation for another,- and Allah knows best what He reveals (in stages),- they say, "Thou art but a forger": but most of them understand not."[10] When Muhammad replaced earlier revelations with new revelations, people called him "a forger." They accused him of making up revelations, because if the Koran is truly the perfect revelation of Allah, there wouldn't be any contradictions. Later revelations would be consistent with earlier revelations. Clearly, the Koran says Allah is all-knowing, so why would Allah need to provide new commands to replace earlier ones? While Allah said "Let there be no compulsion in religion,"[11] the Koran also records Allah saying "I will instil terror into the hearts of the Unbelievers: smite ye above their necks and smite all their finger-tips off them."[12] So, are Muslims supposed to be at peace with non-Muslims, or are they supposed to cut off their heads?

Well, later revelations are some of the most violent passages in the Koran. In Chapter 9 of the Koran, one of the final revelations of Allah, believers are commanded to "Fight those who believe not in Allah…until they pay the Jizya with willing submission, and feel themselves subdued."[13] The 'Jizya' is a tax non-Muslims are forced to pay for not converting to Islam. Since later revelations replace earlier revelations, the Koran's violent passages replace the non-violent passages. Fortunately, not all Muslims agree with abrogation, so they choose not to accept the revelations in Islam that command violence toward non-Muslims. Still, if the earlier revelations recorded in the Koran have the same authority as the later revelations, why are there so many discrepancies between them? Regardless, despite commanding violence toward non-Muslims, the Koran also says Christians and Muslims worship the same God.[14] Of course, if this is true, why is the God of the Bible so different from Allah?

For example, the Koran denies Jesus is God,[15] while the Holy Bible teaches Jesus is God.[16] Muslims and Christians definitely don't worship the same God. Yet, while the Koran denies that Jesus is God, it also clearly shows Jesus is God. The Koran says only Allah can give life.[17] Besides Allah, no one can "create (even) a fly."[18] According to the Koran, however, Jesus did better than a fly. The Koran claims Jesus said "I make for you out of clay, as it were, the figure of a bird, and breathe into it, and it becomes a bird by Allah's leave."[19] Not only does the Koran say the Lord Jesus created a bird and gave it life, He also raised the dead. The Koran says Jesus "bringest forth the dead."[20] In other words, only Allah can create and give life, but the Koran says the Jesus created and gave life. This may explain why the Koran calls Allah "the Best of Creators."[21] How can it be that Allah is the best of creators, if only Allah can create? Well, as reported by the Koran, Jesus has the title of Creator. Strangely, though the Koran says Jesus is Creator, it firmly denies He is God. This is far from the only difference between the God of the Bible and Allah.

The Holy Bible says God wants to be known.[22] The Lord Jesus added a human nature to His divine nature so that by Him we might see the fullness of God.[23] On the other hand, the Koran says Allah is completely unknowable.[24] How can people know anything about something that is unknowable? Muslims have tried to describe Allah's nature, but how can anyone describe something that can't be known? In addition to being unknowable, the Koran says Allah is an impersonal, singular entity.[25]

So, since Allah is impersonal and singular, how can Allah have the attribute of love? Before we were created, who did Allah love? Love needs at least two people. There must be a person who loves and an object of that person's love. Impersonal entities aren't capable of love, so how could a non-loving impersonal entity create loving, personal beings? Certainly, the Koran describes Allah as merciful and affectionate,[26] but how does an impersonal entity show mercy and affection? How can an unknowable entity be described at all?

Unlike the Koran, the Holy Bible says "God is love."[27] The true God of the universe exists in three distinct, co-equal Persons: Father, Son, and Holy Spirit. There isn't one person and three persons, or one god and three gods. God is three-in-one. Love is an eternal attribute of God because there has always been a loving relationship between the Father, the Son and the Holy Spirit. God is love, and the Bible says we love because He first loved us.[28] By making us in His image, God has given us the ability to love. Husbands love their wives, parents love their children, and brothers love their sisters.

We have relationships because God is personal and relational, and we are made in His image. Since Allah is an impersonal entity, and doesn't have the attribute of love, how could Allah have created humans with the ability to love?

By contrast, the Father loved the world so much, He sent God the Son to suffer the penalty for our rebellion against Him. God is perfectly just, so He must punish our rebellion. The sacrificial death of Jesus Christ satisfied God's justice, while allowing Him to show us mercy. Allah, however, isn't perfectly just. To be perfectly just, Allah would have to punish all sin. The Koran says "Allah is never unjust in the least degree,"[29] but it also says Allah is "Most Merciful."[30] If Allah forgives people without any punishment for their sins, justice isn't served. In fact, the Koran says "those whose balance (of good deeds) is heavy,- they will attain salvation: But those whose balance is light, will be those who have lost their souls."[31] This isn't justice.

For starters, good deeds don't remove bad deeds. Judges don't let murderers go free because they volunteer at a soup kitchen every now and then. More importantly, if a criminal was freed because the criminal did something the judge liked, the judge would be accepting a bribe. Good deeds are an attempt to make a judge overlook a crime. Put differently, good deeds are a bribe, and no righteous judge would accept a bribe. So, why would Allah show favoritism to certain people for doing deeds he liked, while punishing others because they didn't do enough of the deeds he liked?

As a result, Muslims can't be certain of what will happen to them when they die. How can they know if they're doing enough good deeds? Even Muhammad, who Allah chose to give his revelation to, said "nor do I know what will be done with me or with you."[32] After all, the Koran also says "Every soul that hath sinned, if it possessed all that is on earth, would fain give it in ransom."[33] In other words, if a man possessed everything on earth and offered it to Allah as a sacrifice for his sins, it wouldn't be enough for his sins to be forgiven. If someone breaks the law, and has to pay a fine, a righteous judge won't let that person go. Justice must be served. It doesn't matter how sorry the law-breaker is, or how many good deeds they've done. Someone must pay the fine.

The God of the Bible is perfectly just. Only God is perfect and without sin, so the Son of God added a human nature to His divine nature to pay the penalty for our sin. The sacrificial death of Jesus satisfied the perfect justice of God, and enabled God to show us mercy. Of course, Muslims don't believe Jesus died. The Koran records people saying "We killed Christ Jesus the son of Mary, the Apostle of God," and then adds "but they killed him not, nor crucified him, but so it was made to appear to them."[34] According to the Koran, Allah tricked people into thinking Jesus Christ was crucified. Allah deceived people by making it appear that Jesus had died.

Since Allah is a deceiver, how could anything in the Koran be trusted? How do Muslims know Allah hasn't deceived them? Allah "leaves straying those whom He pleases and guides whom He pleases,"[35] so how can anyone know when Allah is leading them astray or not? After all, the Koran claims Jesus Christ miraculously spoke as an infant "peace is on me the day I was born, the day that I die, and the day that I shall be raised up to life."[36] So, the Koran says Jesus Christ died, but it also says "for of a surety they killed him not:- Nay, Allah raised him up unto Himself."[37] Did Jesus die, or did Allah take Him up into Heaven? Well, whenever there is a doubt about something in the Koran, Muslims are supposed to look to the Holy Bible. The Koran instructs Muslims "If thou wert in doubt as to what We have revealed unto thee, then ask those who have been reading the Book from before thee: the Truth hath indeed come to thee from thy Lord: so be in no wise of those in doubt."[38]

The Bible is quite clear: Jesus suffered death by crucifixion to pay the penalty for our sins.[39] He rose again, showing His power over all things, including death.[40] The Father accepted the sacrificial death of the Son as the full payment for our sins. The death of Jesus Christ fully paid for our sins, and His Resurrection was the guarantee our sins had been fully paid for. On the other hand, Allah didn't die for anyone. Being completely impersonal, and entirely unknowable, how could Allah even relate to anybody? Allah didn't send anyone to pay the penalty for our sins, but then, the Koran says there is no need for justice to be served. If people do enough good deeds, their sins might be overlooked by Allah. There is no guarantee, but maybe the good deeds will sway Allah to show mercy.

The one true God, however, loves us so much He sent His Son to pay the penalty for our sins. While Allah's chosen messenger Muhammad died, and remained lifeless in the grave, Jesus is alive. He has always been and He always will be. He added a human nature to die for us, but He is alive forevermore. Muhammad, Allah's chosen messenger, was unable to perform miracles.[41] Yet, even the Koran records that the Lord Jesus performed miracles.[42] The Koran asks "Who can give life to (dry) bones and decomposed ones (at that)?"[43] The Koran answers its own question, stating Jesus "bringest forth the dead."[44] While Muhammad was a sinner,[45] who had no clue what would happen to him when he died,[46] the Koran says Jesus Christ is sinless[47] and living in Heaven.[48]

Naturally, because Jesus is without sin, He never lied. The Koran also says the Holy Bible is the perfect revelation of Allah,[49] and the words of Allah can never change or be corrupted.[50] Since Jesus Christ never lied, and the Holy Bible is perfect and incorruptible, everything the Bible records Jesus saying is completely true. Well, the Holy Bible records Jesus Christ saying "I am the way, the truth, and the life: no man cometh unto the Father, but by me."[51] In other words, the only way to Heaven is through Jesus Christ. All Muslims, according to their very own Korans, should be Christians.

Now, it's no secret Muhammad said "Whoever changes his Islamic religion, kill him."[52] With all due respect, the true Word of God says not to worry. What can man do? Jesus Christ said if you are persecuted for His sake, you should be glad, "for great is your reward in heaven."[53] Christians have nothing to fear, because they believe in the one true God of the universe. Of course, calling yourself a Christian doesn't mean you are one.

Cults

If you've ever encountered a couple of clean-cut well-dressed people on your doorstep with name badges and some flashy religious materials, you're probably familiar with non-Christian cults. These days, the term 'cult' has fallen out of favor. It's just so impolite, but then, so is identity theft. After all, non-Christian cults reject Christian beliefs, while simultaneously claiming to be Christians. It's better to be biblically correct than politically correct, so what's a non-Christian cult all about?

Well, it's simple mathematics. Cults will always subtract from the Person of Jesus Christ, denying He is God and making Him equal to or less than the spiritual leader of their group. Likewise, cults will always add to the Word of the God. They have their own extra-special writings that are believed to be superior to the Bible. In addition, cults will multiply the number of things you have to do to be saved from your sins. While the Bible clearly says the sacrificial death of Jesus Christ fully paid for your sins, cults usually add quite a lot of other deeds to the equation. Finally, at the head of every cult is a charismatic founder or leader. Joseph Smith Jr. founded the Mormon Church, while the Jehovah's Witnesses began with Charles T. Russell. Like all leaders of non-Christian cults, they believed in a god that was far different from the God of the Bible.

For the most part, non-Christian cults believe Jesus was nothing more than a good man. Jesus disagreed, and good men don't lie. He once told a crowd "I and my Father are one."[54] When the crowd heard Jesus say this, they wanted to stone Him to death. They said they were going to stone Him "for blasphemy; and because that thou, being a man, makest thyself God."[55] The crowd clearly understood what Jesus was saying. After all, facing death, Jesus didn't tell them they had misunderstood. They understood His words correctly, and they didn't like what He was saying. They didn't believe "God was manifest in the flesh."[56] Similarly, Jesus didn't correct Thomas when he worshipfully proclaimed "My LORD and my God."[57] Thomas wasn't using God's name as a curse word. On the contrary, he was simply telling it like it is. Jesus confirmed this by telling Thomas "because thou hast seen me, thou hast believed: blessed are they that have not seen, and yet have believed."[58]

Still, some people have objections. Often, people point out Jesus said "my Father is greater than I."[59] Well, Jesus didn't say the Father was different, superior or better. Instead, He was talking about the Father's greater position in Heaven. By coming to earth, Jesus had to add a human nature to His divine nature. He had to be fully human so He could fully experience humanity, including death on a cross. By adding a human nature, He temporarily assumed a lower position than the Father in Heaven. This is why Jesus Christ also said during His time on earth that "I and my Father are one." By adding a human nature, Jesus never stopped being God.

While on earth, however, Jesus only exercised His divine powers with the Father's authority. Indeed, He stated "The Son can do nothing of himself, but what he seeth the Father do: for what things soever he doeth, these also doeth the Son likewise."[60] He was completely obedient to the will of the Father. As a result, in His humanity, Jesus didn't know the day or hour of His return.[61] It was the Father's privilege to withhold that information. Jesus was completely dependent upon the Father, which is why He prayed to Him, setting the example of obedience for us to follow. In His divinity, however, Jesus knew all things. This is why His followers said to Him "Lord, thou knowest all things."[62]

Jesus didn't correct them, because they were telling it like it is. Jesus Christ is all-knowing. On earth, He could, and did, exercise His divine powers in accordance with the will of the Father.

After all, Jesus is "the image of the invisible God, the firstborn of every creature."[63] Firstborn doesn't mean first created. On the contrary, it means first in rank. The Lord Jesus is supreme over all of His creation, "For by him all things were created."[64] Jesus, the image of the invisible God, said "he that hath seen me hath seen the Father."[65] The Bible records that the enemies of Jesus "sought the more to kill him" because He "said also that God was his Father, making himself equal with God."[66] Additionally, the enemies of Jesus said "We have a law, and by our law he ought to die, because he made himself the Son of God."[67] Being the 'son of' meant 'having the same nature of.' Jesus Christ is the unique Son of God, because He is by nature God. Even His enemies acknowledged He claimed to be God, they just chose not to believe Him.

While most non-Christian cults believe Jesus was just a man, there are a few exceptions. The Church of Jesus Christ of Latter-day Saints, or Mormons for short, maintains Jesus is the brother of Satan[68] and one of many 'gods.'[69] They believe Jesus is the product of a union between the Father and His 'goddess' wife.[70] According to Mormons, the Father was once a man on another planet, until He became a 'god.'[71] Jesus is a separate 'god,' and Mormons can also become 'gods' if they live good lives.[72] What does the Bible have to say about all of this?

For starters, although Mormons believe in many gods, the Bible teaches there is only one God.[73] The Bible records God saying "before me there was no God formed, neither shall there be after me."[74] Curiously, the Book of Mormon teaches the same thing. In Alma 11:26-29, we read "And Zeezrom said unto him: Thou sayest there is a true and living God? And Amulek said: Yea, there is a true and living God. Now Zeezrom said: Is there more than one God? And he answered, No."[75] Wild names aside, that's pretty straightforward. In other words, the Bible and the Book of Mormon both teach there is only one God, but Mormons believe there are many gods. What's that all about?

Likewise, the Mormon belief that God was once a man on another planet isn't supported by the Bible, or the Book of Mormon. Sure, Joseph Smith claimed "God himself was once as we are now, and is an exalted man." He even added "We have imagined that God was God from all eternity. I will refute that idea and take away the veil, so that you may see."[76] Yet, the Bible says "Before the mountains were brought forth, or ever thou hadst formed the earth and the world, even from everlasting to everlasting, thou art God."[77] Strangely, the Book of Mormon is in perfect agreement, stating "God is not a partial God, neither a changeable being; but he is unchangeable from all eternity to all eternity."[78] Apparently, Joseph Smith intended to refute his own Book of Mormon. Put differently, both the Bible and the Book of Mormon teach that God is eternal and unchangeable, but Mormons say the Father was once a man who became a 'god.' Something just isn't adding up.

Of course, since the Bible repeatedly says Jesus is God,[79] Jesus must've always been God. Indeed, the Bible says "All things were made by him."[80] Jesus created all things, including Satan. Jehovah's Witnesses, however, beg to differ. They think Jesus is Michael the Archangel[81] and a lesser 'god'[82] who became a man. The Watchtower Society, the corporate arm of Jehovah's Witnesses, produces a rather imaginative 'translation' of the Bible called the *New World Translation of the Holy Scriptures*. In it, they've made a number of changes to the text to support their anti-biblical beliefs.

For example, they've changed John 1:1-3 to say that Jesus Christ is a 'god,' instead of God. This could mean one of two things. It could mean Jehovah's Witnesses believe Jesus is a false 'god' like Satan, but it's more likely they believe Jesus is a separate, lesser 'god.' So, like Mormons, Jehovah's Witnesses believe in many 'gods.' Again, the Bible repeatedly states there is only one true God. Besides, John 1:3 says of Jesus that "without him nothing was made that has been made."[83] If Jesus is an angel who became a man, He would be a created being. So, if Jesus created everything and He's a created being, did Jesus create Himself? According to Jehovah's Witnesses, Jesus is self-created, but how does something that doesn't exist create itself?

On top of that, the Bible says Jesus is "the express image" of God.[84] If Jesus was an angel who became a man, how could He be the exact image of God? Incidentally, where in the Bible is Jesus actually called Michael the Archangel? Five verses in the Bible mention Michael.[85] None of them call Him Jesus, not even in the Jehovah's Witnesses 'translation' of the Bible. Quite the opposite, Michael is called "one of the chief princes"[86] while Jesus is called "Lord of lords and King of kings."[87] In addition, the Bible says Michael once told Satan, "The Lord rebuke thee."[88] If Michael was Lord of lords, as Jesus is, why would he say 'The Lord rebuke thee'? Why didn't he rebuke him personally? After all, Jesus displayed His authority over Satan when He told him to get lost.[89] Jesus rebuked Satan to his face, and Satan immediately fled.[90]

To get around these stumbling blocks, Jehovah's Witnesses will often say "But Jesus is coming back with the voice of the archangel, so He must be an archangel!" Certainly, the Bible says Jesus will return to the earth "with the voice of the archangel, and with the trump of God."[91] That said, the expression "with the voice of the archangel" means that the archangel, like God's trumpet, will announce the coming of the Lord. The verse doesn't say the Lord Jesus is an archangel, or God's trumpet for that matter. He's Lord of lords and King of kings. Still, Jehovah's Witnesses might object, "Why does the Bible say Jesus is the only begotten Son?"[92]

Well, the word 'begotten' is an English translation of a Greek word which means 'one of a kind.'[93] Again, to be the 'son of' meant 'having the same nature of,' so Jesus is the one and only Son of God. He isn't begotten in the sense of being physically created. Interestingly enough, a different Greek word is also translated 'begotten' in the Bible when talking about Jesus. Psalm 2:7 records God saying "Thou art my Son; this day have I begotten thee."[94] This is a translation of a Greek word which means 'brought forth.'[95] This verse is cited three times in the New Testament to speak of the Resurrection.[96] Psalm 2:7, then, is a fulfilled prophecy of Jesus being 'brought forth' from the grave. Through the Resurrection, Jesus was "declared to be the Son of God with power."[97] The Resurrection was the public declaration of Jesus' true identity as the Son of God. By the way, this is really good news, because the Bible teaches only God can save.[98] If only God can save, how could a created angel who became a man save anybody? It just wouldn't work.

Fortunately, the Bible states Jesus is "the great God and our Saviour"[99] despite the objections of Jehovah's Witnesses. The Bible also teaches that the Holy Spirit is God, rather than an impersonal 'force' like Jehovah's Witnesses believe. First off, the Holy Spirit is called God several times in the Bible.[100] Additionally, the Bible records "the Spirit said unto Philip, Go near"[101] and "the Holy Ghost said, Separate me Barnabas and Saul for the work whereunto I have called them."[102] If the Holy Spirit is an impersonal force, how can He speak?[103] The Holy Spirit can also be grieved[104] and insulted.[105] How can an impersonal force be grieved and insulted? The Bible says the Holy Spirit is eternal,[106] all-powerful,[107] all-knowing[108] and Creator.[109] In addition, the Bible records a man lying to the Holy Spirit.[110] How could someone lie to a force? The man didn't lie to a force, however, because the Bible notes he had "not lied unto men, but unto God."[111] The Holy Spirit is God, just as the Son is God. While Seventh-day Adventists agree about the Holy Spirit, they aren't quite sure about the identity of the Son.

On the one hand, Seventh-day Adventists believe Jesus is fully God. On the other hand, they believe everything Ellen G. White said was perfectly inspired of God.[112] This is a bit problematic, because Ellen G. White frequently contradicted the Bible. In fact, she once stated "Jesus was revealed to them as the Angel of Jehovah, the Captain of the Lord's Host, Michael the Archangel."[113] As a result, Seventh-day Adventists must believe Jesus is somehow God and Michael the Archangel at the same time. How could Jesus be the Creator of the universe and a created being at the same time? It's tough to say, so Seventh-day Adventists claim 'Michael' is just another title for Jesus. Again, Michael is never called Jesus in the Bible, and Jesus is never called Michael. To make their case, they usually state that the name 'Michael' means 'one who is like God.' A more accurate translation would be 'who is like God?' but that's neither here nor there. Jesus isn't like God. He is God. Indeed, one of His actual titles is Immanuel, which means 'God with us.'[114] Jesus can't be God and a created being at the same time, but this is what Ellen G. White taught. She said "The man Christ Jesus was not the Lord God Almighty, yet Christ and the Father are one."[115] It's all rather confusing, but fortunately, the Bible is very clear about the real identity of Jesus Christ.

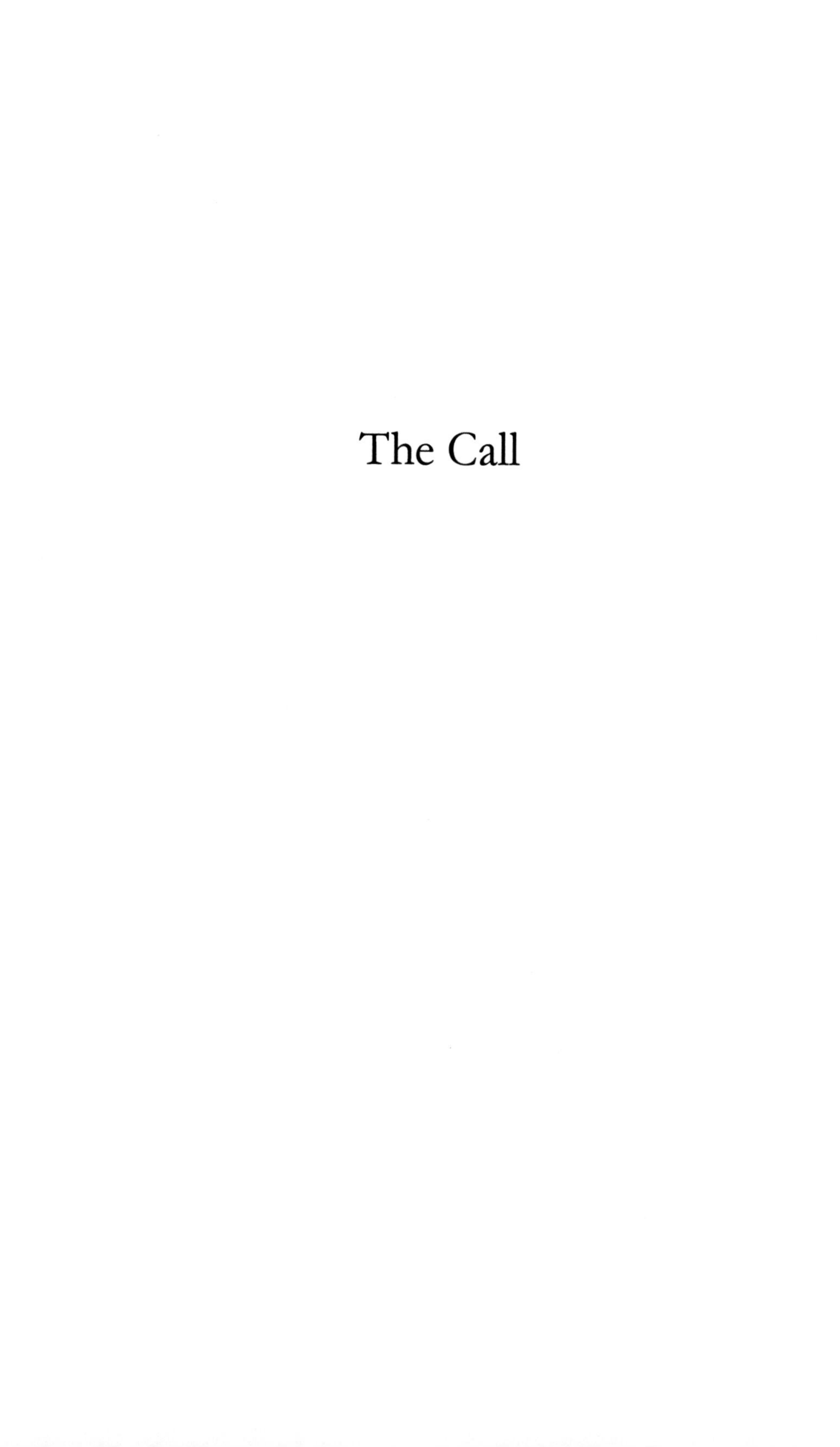

The Call

There is nothing new under the sun.[1] Sure, inventions may crop up, but everything ever made by human beings was formed from materials of the earth. In time, the works of human hands are often forgotten, having been replaced with something that performs a similar function and uses the same materials. It's all been done before. Generations come and go, but there remains an appointed time for everything. Everyone experiences times of happiness and sorrow, times of success and struggle. Whether good or bad, our experiences don't last forever. There comes a time when everybody dies. It's the same the world over. The deceased leave behind everyone they've loved and everything they've worked for. It has been so for generations past and present, and so it has left countless people wondering: why am I here?

Well, if evolution is true, there is no God. Life would be meaningless. Take a look around. Injustice is everywhere. People get away with crimes all the time, but what use would it be to speak of justice, if there is no absolute standard of right and wrong? If there is no God, justice is a matter of personal preference. It's just one person's opinion against the opinion of someone else, so why have courts? Why should people be put in jail for 'crimes,' when according to their moral code, they've done nothing wrong? There'd be no reason to have laws at all. Who could possibly tell another person what is definitively right and wrong? Why should we trust one person's opinion over the opinion of others?

Besides, if matter is all there is, people could hardly be held responsible for the so-called crimes they commit. Thoughts would simply be the result of chemical reactions in the brain. So, why punish people who can't help the crimes they commit? We don't put cars behind bars when they break down, so why do the same when people's atoms start acting up? Yet, many individuals are angry when criminals get away with murder. They're mad when justice isn't served, but why should they be? It's not as if victims have rights.

Indeed, if there is no Creator, nobody has rights from birth. Would humans be any different from a blade of grass? Did we not come from the same pond chemicals as every other living organism on the planet? Why would we have 'rights'? Perhaps, privileges that are called 'rights' could be given and taken away by the government. You better hope the ruling party is generous. Regardless, privileges and rights wouldn't really have meaning, because humans wouldn't have free will anyway. Our actions would all be the result of predetermined chemical reactions in the brain. We'd have no control over them. As a result, it wouldn't make sense to talk about freedom, because no one would be free to do anything.

Still, people feel strongly about justice and individual rights. It bothers people that criminals repeatedly walk free, and personal rights are constantly violated. These are the facts of life, and many people try to avoid thinking about such depressing matters. They usually turn to possessions and pleasures to take their mind of widespread injustices, but what fulfillment can they bring? Money is a great tool, but the more you make, the more worries you'll have. No matter how much you have, you will never find satisfaction. How much is enough? To make matters worse, when you die, you'll leave everything you worked for behind. All of your wealth will be in someone else's hands. Since you can't take your money and possessions with you, what's the point of working so hard for them? On top of that, why bother going to class? What would being the richest, smartest person in the cemetery accomplish?

With this in mind, a lot of people turn to drugs, sex and other pleasures. For a time, these pursuits might be enjoyable, but the fun never lasts. It's all temporary. Reality always sets back in. Soon enough, people can't even find past pleasures enjoyable. There is no one lonelier in this world than someone weary of pleasure. The workaholic can never have enough time, and the pleasure-seeker can never have enough time off. Eventually, time runs out for all of us.

Everybody dies, and without God, no one can know what happens after death. From what we observe, it isn't pretty. Does everything fade to black? Do we only live once? Surely, many desperate people have ended their lives because they hoped this was true. They couldn't take the pain, frustration and sorrow of this world any longer. Meanwhile, the loved ones of the deceased grieve, but only for a time. As the years pass, they'll move on. Most people are forgotten within a generation. For the people who are remembered, they aren't alive to see their legacy, so what does it matter?

Without a doubt, if evolution is true, life is a most cruel accident. Love, joy, courage, generosity and kindness would be nothing more than predetermined chemical reactions in the brain. Every activity would be meaningless, because everything fades away. What point would there be in waking up every day? Nothing lasts and nothing can bring fulfillment. Even words would be without meaning. What use would it be to talk about 'good' and 'evil'? What is evil for one person might be good for someone else, and no opinion could be more right or wrong than that of another. There would be no satisfaction. Who could ever have their fill of hearing and seeing, tasting and touching? All the while, the uncertainty of death remains.

How would we know evolution is true? Simply put, we couldn't. If evolution is true, no one could know if anything is true. 'Thoughts' would be chemically sound, not logically sound, so why trust them? Naturally, no one could answer the 'why' question, let alone the question of how we got here. Of course, this hasn't stopped people from speculating. After all, evolution is a theory of history that attempts to explain the origin of life. Without an eyewitness account, however, who can know how everything began?

Clearly, evolution must be accepted by a leap of faith. Let's recap. No one observed how nothing made matter, in spite of the First Law of Thermodynamics. Nobody saw how non-living chemicals gave rise to a living single-celled organism, in spite of the Law of Biogenesis. There were no witnesses when natural selection, which reduces genetic information over time, somehow made a one-celled organism become more complex. How could anyone know how these 'unscientific' events happened?

On the other hand, the Holy Bible is a reliable eyewitness account of how we got here, why we're here and why the world is the way it is. In the beginning, God created a perfect world, but this is certainly not how we find it today. Due to Adam and Eve's rebellion against God, suffering and death entered the world. Upon disobeying, they immediately died spiritually and began to die physically from that day forward. As a result, everybody is born in a broken state, in a broken world, and in a broken relationship with God. All of us have inherited Adam's sinful nature, separated from God at birth, suffering the effects of human sin and separation from God throughout our lives.

We all have a God-shaped hole in our heart.

Sadly, many people spend their entire lives trying to fill this void with anything but God. The human heart is restless, always seeking but never finding rest in the things of this world. People try business, family, entertainment, sports, politics, drugs, wealth, sex and anything other than God, but nothing satisfies. A measure of happiness might be achieved for a time, but all the success, riches, popularity and power never last. Usually, the things of the world fall miserably short of expectations. People have their hopes set on some new possession, hobby, activity or person to be life-changing, but nothing lives up to the hype. Everything falls short. All things disappoint.

Every now and then, people wonder in frustration why their lives aren't more fulfilling. The things of this world promise to satisfy, but they never deliver. How much is enough? Everything loses its shine, and someone else always has something that seems better at the time. Success, riches and popularity bring enemies, worries and the sacrifice of principles. The more ambitions, the more work, and who can take the fruit of their labors with them when they pass away? When the things of this world disappoint, emptiness sets in. People feel hollow instead of whole. Often, they turn to alcohol and drugs to numb the pain, but these substances soon become a powerful source of suffering in their own right. Before long, people are slaves to their desires and addictions. There is the way things should be and the way things actually are, and the two rarely meet. People always think they can control themselves and their situation, but human control has its limits. Who can know what tomorrow will bring? All the while, people are left thinking there must be more to life. Surely, this can't be what it's all about.

Like a square peg can't fit into a round hole, our God-shaped hole can't be filled with something other than God. Even worldly religion won't get the job done. Only a personal relationship with God through Jesus Christ can satisfy. Jesus is the only way to a restored relationship with God. For the most part, though, people would rather reject God and continue living by their own rules. Since the punishment for their wrongdoing isn't quickly carried out, they think it is safe to do wrong. While their punishment may not be immediate, it is sure to come.

God is perfectly just. He must punish sin. Not long after the rebellion of Adam and Eve, the world was filled with evil. God judged the wickedness of the human race by sending a catastrophic global flood. Just as there was a global judgment by water, there is a coming judgment by fire.[2] Fortunately, while God is just, He is also merciful. By faith, Noah and his family were saved by the Ark, a massive ship with no rudder and no steering wheel of any kind. God was the Pilot, and the Ark saved everyone who entered through its only door. Likewise, to escape the coming judgment by fire, everyone must enter through a door. Jesus said, "I am the door: by me if any man enter in, he shall be saved."[3] Jesus Christ is the Ark of salvation today, and only through Him can people be saved.

Unfortunately, as it was in the days of Noah, most people laugh at the idea of God's judgment. For years, the people of Noah's day could've boarded the Ark. They chose to continue living by their own rules, openly rebelling against God. Instead of trusting in God by walking through the door, they made fun of the Ark. It was a punch line. Although there was more than enough room, no one decided to join Noah and his family on the Ark. Quite likely, they thought Noah was out of his mind. Tragically, they were too absorbed with the things of this world. The people of Noah's day were looking to fill their God-shaped hole with anything but God. They were searching for fulfillment, and it could only be found on the very Ark they mocked. The Ark stood as a warning of coming judgment, but the people of Noah's day couldn't be bothered.

While the door of the Ark was open, anyone could enter and be saved. Once God shut the door, no one else could come aboard. Before the Flood, everyone went about life as usual. By the time the floodwaters came, it was too late. Everyone who ridiculed the Ark tried to dog paddle their way to salvation, but it didn't work out the way they hoped. It is no different today. Unless people believe they will be held accountable for their actions, they will do as they please. Naturally, humans don't want to believe they will be judged, because everyone wants to continue living by their own rules. Since the ultimate punishment for their rebellion doesn't take place in their lifetime, they think they will get away with it. Other people think their good deeds will be enough to acquit them, but God cannot be bribed. All sin must be punished. That's the reality of it. Justice must be served. Nobody wants to believe they'll be judged for their sins, but it doesn't matter if anyone believes it or not. God will punish sin. People didn't think the Flood would come. They didn't think they would be judged, but their belief didn't prevent them from drowning. Believing something doesn't make it true, and trying to replace God doesn't make Him disappear.

Unsurprisingly, this hasn't stopped people's efforts to remove God from public view, and replace Him with something they find less threatening. The more things change, the more they stay the same. Certainly, Noah's descendants were no strangers to this strategy. They didn't want to spread out and fill the earth, as God had commanded. They didn't like God telling them what to do. So, they rebelled. To help suppress their guilt, they tried to replace God. Instead of defending their sins, they removed the idea of sin altogether. They put their hands over their ears and pretended God wasn't there. Yet, when replacing God, they wanted to retain some sort of spirituality. They tried to fill their God-shaped hole with anything but God. At Babel, Noah's descendants went about building a tall tower they thought could bridge the gap between the physical world and the spiritual world, without the need for God. They looked to the position of the planets and the stars for guidance and fulfillment in their lives. It is no different today.

Everybody wants spirituality without truth. It's all the rage, but it's all been done before. Like at Babel, people serve the creation rather than the Creator. Everyone worships something. When people remove God from their lives, the object of their worship will always be something inferior. They worship their possessions, their careers, their families, their favorite teams and other created things. These things never last, and they always bring frustration and disappointment. Even so, most people make them the purpose of their existence. These days, the environment has become a popular object of worship, but this is quite problematic.

First off, the environment is far from perfect. Nature is filled with pain, suffering and death. Why would anyone worship something with so much evil? Regardless, many people believe nature is perfect anyway. If this is true, however, no one would have the right to meddle in nature. In other words, recycling and composting would be crimes against the earth. By trying to interfere with the natural process, environmentalism would be high treason against the environment's perfect workings. To be fair, if humans are just highly evolved animals which came from pond chemicals, we would be just as natural as the rest of the world.

Certainly, if evolution is true, at what point did humans become different from other animals? When did our pollution become 'unnatural'? Who decides what's 'natural' and 'unnatural' anyway? Why would our use of resources be any different from the consumption patterns of other animals? Besides, if life is all about passing our genes on to the next generation, why would humans consume fewer resources? If nature is all there is, human behavior would be just as 'natural' as the behavior of any other animal. Since all living things would have come from the same pond chemicals, humans would be no different from animals.

Indeed, human beings would have the same worth as plants and animals. There would be no rights, no laws, no freedom and no dignity. That said, people who worship nature usually consider plant and animal life to be sacred. If this is true, 'moral' human beings would starve to death. Since we would all be related, eating an apple would be murder and cannibalism. Why would anyone have the right to step on grass or cut down trees? Wouldn't that be violating their rights and their dignity?

Clearly, if nature is all there is, all life is either equally sacred or equally worthless. Which view is correct? It's up to personal preference, which is precisely why God is rejected in the first place. No matter what created thing people worship, they reject God because they don't want to be accountable to Him. To fill their longing for meaning, they look for satisfaction in things that don't condemn their lifestyle. Predictably, whenever they hear anything about the God of the Bible, they throw a tantrum. They demand tolerance, but that's not really what they want.

After all, tolerance is about putting up with something or someone you disagree with. Being tolerant means being respectful of beliefs you don't approve of. Today, most people think tolerance means accepting that all beliefs are true. Whenever someone mentions the Bible to these individuals, the name-calling begins, because the Bible says all non-Christian beliefs are wrong. Of course, truth is exclusive. If something is true, all other possibilities are false. For example, if a car is completely blue, it can't be another color. The other colors are excluded. Naturally, all truths are absolute. If something is true, it applies to everyone. Gravity doesn't play favorites, and the sum of 2 + 2 is always 4. It doesn't matter what someone's childhood was like or what culture they're from, beliefs can't change the truth. You are free to believe what you want, but what you believe isn't true just because you want it to be.

Now, when people reject Christianity because it is exclusive, they are themselves being exclusive. They are being 'intolerant' by their own definition, because by believing Christianity isn't true, they are saying all beliefs aren't true. Again, tolerance isn't really what people want. On the contrary, they want their lifestyle choices to be legitimized. They don't want others to put up with their wrongdoing; they want others to tell them their behavior is good. Everybody has a conscience, even if most individuals have done their best to suppress it. Everyone knows they are guilty of sin, but no one wants to admit it. As a result, a lot of people try to completely remove God from their lives. They surround themselves with anything and everything but God, because they can't stand the thought of being judged for their sinful behavior.

It isn't enough to reject God. It isn't enough to rebel against Him. Due to their sinfulness, many people simply refuse to even acknowledge God. Some individuals make it their life's work to convince others to do the same. Why do they spend so much time ranting about someone that supposedly doesn't exist? Obviously, they don't spend hours talking about how the Tooth Fairy doesn't exist. Why are they so concerned with trying to convince others God doesn't exist? If He really didn't exist, what difference would it make?

Ultimately, many people rebel against God because they don't like the idea of being judged for their wrongdoing. On top of that, they want to keep living by their own rules, doing as they please without any consequences. They want to be God, so they refuse to acknowledge He exists. They don't want the world to be that way. When they encounter anything related to God, they can't handle it. Consequently, they can't have anyone else acknowledge God, because they don't want to be confronted with the truth they try to suppress. They think if everyone believes God isn't around, there is nothing to worry about. The coast is clear, or so they hope.

Despite their best efforts, it really doesn't matter what people believe. Believing something doesn't make it true. In the end, the truth is inescapable. God will judge sin, and there are only three ways of dealing with this reality. The most common plan of action is to pretend sin doesn't exist, but this doesn't solve the problem. It may make people feel better, but only for a time. The uncertainty of death and the possibility of judgment will haunt them for the rest of their lives. Another popular strategy is to do a lot of good deeds, but nothing can undo bad actions. What's done is done, and all sin must be punished. Whether people think sin doesn't exist or they try to cancel out their wrongdoing, their sin remains. No one wants to hear it, but really, nobody can solve their own sin problem. Only Jesus Christ can.

All of us owe a debt that we can't pay. The rejection in Eden, the rebellion before the Flood and the revolt at Babel are not isolated incidents. Everyone sins, because everyone is a sinner. Everybody has a sin debt, and it grows with each passing day. Well, the Lord Jesus added a human nature to His divine nature to pay our sin debt in full. The Creator became a part of His creation to pay a debt He didn't owe, because we owed a debt we couldn't pay.

In more ways than one, our sin debt is overwhelming. Deep down, everyone is lonely. Family and friends may mask this loneliness much of the time, but it doesn't cure it. In addition, everybody feels guilty. People have regrets about things they've said and done. No amount of drinking, sex and drugs can make guilt disappear. Looming in the distance is the reality of death. Life is short, and everyone knows the clock is ticking. Overall, human beings are lonely because we are born separated from God, guilty because we have disobeyed Him and afraid of dying because we don't want to face Him. It is all too much for us to bear. To be released from our sin debt, we must be born again. Jesus said "Except a man be born again, he cannot see the kingdom of God."[4] He added that everyone "must be born again."[5] What does it mean to be born again?

All of us are born spiritual losers. We are born into a broken world, in a broken condition and in a broken relationship with our Creator. We can't fix ourselves. Only our Creator can. To have a restored relationship with God, we must be born again. When we are born again, we are changed on the inside. It is a spiritual rebirth from above. In other words, the Holy Spirit comes to live inside of you and you become a child of God.[6] Still, if we are born separated from God, how can we enter into a relationship with Him?

The Bible says "the grace of God that bringeth salvation hath appeared to all men."[7] What's so amazing about God's grace? Simply put, it enables us to trust in Jesus. We are freed by God's grace to believe. In our naturally sinful state, we couldn't possibly enter into a relationship with God.[8] Due to our inherited sinfulness, our minds are easily blinded by Satan's deceptions[9] and our hearts love darkness instead of light.[10] Grace enables us to see past the lies of the world and embrace the Light. Likewise, God's grace explains why people aren't as bad as they could be. We naturally want to do the wrong thing, but because of grace we also have the desire to do what's right. Similarly, just as we can choose not to do the right thing, we can choose not to believe.

Faith is a gift because God enables us to believe by His grace, but like other gifts, it can be rejected. God is not to blame for someone's unbelief. He wants everyone to be saved.[11] Indeed, no one can even come to Jesus unless the Father draws them first.[12] Nobody would trust Jesus' claims if it weren't for the many ways in which the Father works to convince people of who Jesus is.[13] Without God's grace, no one could trust in Jesus. Without the Father drawing us to Jesus, no one would trust in Him. Anyone who responds to being lovingly drawn by the Father with faith in Jesus will never be driven away. Jesus said "All that the Father giveth me shall come to me; and him that cometh to me I will in no wise cast out."[14]

In fact, when you believe, you are sealed with the Holy Spirit.[15] The Holy Spirit comes to live inside of you and you are born again. Your God-shaped hole is filled. Loneliness is replaced with joy. Guilt is healed. The heart is mended, and your old ways pass away. Truly, you will become a new creation. The Holy Spirit will enable you to act more like Jesus Christ. Will you be perfect? Absolutely not, but you will want to be. This doesn't mean you have to religiously follow a bunch of rules. Christianity only has two rules. Jesus commanded His followers to love God with all of our heart, soul, mind and strength, and to love our neighbor as ourselves.[16] That's it. A person who is truly born again has an intimate relationship with God.

Contrary to popular belief, only people who are born again are Christians. Being baptized, going to church and reading the Bible are all good things, but they won't make you a Christian. It isn't something that can be earned. In addition, you can't be neutral about Jesus. He didn't give us that option. Jesus said "He that is not with me is against me."[17] Truly, to be saved from the coming judgment, you must be born again.

Yes, Jesus is coming back. He will set everything right, judging rebellion against Him and restoring all things. Why hasn't He come back yet? Well, out of love, God is giving everyone a chance to trust in Him. He doesn't want anyone to be judged for their sins against Him, so He is giving everybody time to change their mind about their sins.[18] This grace period won't last forever. Anyone that isn't with Jesus is against Him, and they will be called to account for their sin debt. Yet, out of His love, God has warned us beforehand of the decision we all face. Will we put our trust in man, or will we put our trust in Him?

Over 1,900 years ago, the Bible predicted that before Jesus came back, a single man will have total control of the world. This coming global dictator is known as the Antichrist.[19] He will be a proud hater of God,[20] relentlessly persecuting Christians[21] and the Jewish people.[22] He will seduce many people, "but not by his own power."[23] Satan will give his power and authority to the Antichrist.[24] He's going to be the height of Satan's deceptive mimicry, a convincing counterfeit that will deceive many people. His coming will even be marked by false miracles to deceive people into believing he is God.[25] In time, this world is going to get a whole lot stranger. UFOs and 'alien abductions' are just the tip of the iceberg. Jesus said "For there shall arise false Christs, and false prophets, and shall shew great signs and wonders; insomuch that, if it were possible, they shall deceive the very elect."[26] The 'very elect' refers to Christians. Election is conditional on faith in Jesus Christ. The

Bible says everyone who trusts in Jesus for the forgiveness of their sins is chosen by the Father to be saved.[27] There is security from deception in Jesus alone, and just before He returns, Satan's puppet ruler will have total control of a global economy.

To buy and sell, everyone will have "to receive a mark in their right hand, or in their foreheads."[28] People that don't take this mark won't be able to work, buy and sell.[29] Of course, only in recent years has tracking financial transactions on such a large scale become possible. Laser technology, barcodes and radio-frequency identification microchips have made a mark in the skin that holds financial information quite plausible. On top of that, with credit cards, debit cards, direct deposit and electronic funds withdrawal, cash is quickly becoming a thing of the past. Clearly, the technology for a one-world economy is here. Unfortunately, the technology for global war is also here. Indeed, Jesus said a sign of His near return would be "wars and rumours of wars."[30]

Still, many people think there is a way to put an end to all violent conflicts. They suggest world peace is obtainable, but it can only come through world government. While the majority of conflicts are between nations, some wars are fought for religious reasons. Naturally, to completely have world peace, they maintain there must also be a global religion. If this sounds familiar, it's because it has already been tried before.

As it was at Babel, so it will be in the final days before the coming of the Lord Jesus. Just as God judged the revolt at Babel, so He will judge the coming one-world system. At Babel, His judgment served a loving purpose. God stopped the rebellion before it went too far, like it had in the days of Noah. His judgment intended to shatter the myth that human beings are able to live their lives by their own rules without any consequences. He caused confusion and division to make them realize their need for Him. They stood condemned before God because of their sin. Out of mercy, He frustrated their plans so that they might change their mind about their sins and trust in Him. He was giving them more time to be saved from eternal condemnation, but time runs out for everybody.

While God is giving everyone plenty of time to be saved, eventually, He will judge the human race once and for all. By far, the greatest problem facing the human race is sin, and it has eternal consequences. Violence in the world is tragic, but it's all the result of sin. No amount of legislation can change the human heart. No matter what humans try to do, there won't be world peace until Jesus comes back. Ultimately, however, world government isn't about ending conflicts. Likewise, global religion isn't about freedom from intolerance. The purpose of a world government and a global religion is to obtain peace of mind. By removing God from everybody's lives, as it was at Babel, sinful humans will convince themselves they are free to live by their own rules.

Needless to say, this won't solve their sin problem. Beliefs don't change the truth. The weight of their sin debt will not be lifted, but they will try to pretend it isn't there. Their nagging guilt won't go away, but they will do their best to suppress it. They will try to smother any doubts, but the idea they might be wrong will terrify them. All told, Jesus Christ is the only way to have peace of mind, but trusting in Him is a no-no for most people. They don't want to give up their lifestyles. Since they don't want to be reminded of God at all, they hate anything remotely related to Him. Over the years, one man's trust in God has been the source of a lot of this hatred.

Roughly 4,000 years ago, God made a promise to a man named Abraham. Due to his faith, God told him "I will make of thee a great nation, and I will bless thee, and make thy name great; and thou shalt be a blessing: And I will bless them that bless thee, and curse him that curseth thee: and in thee shall all families of the earth be blessed."[31] This promise was reaffirmed to Abraham's son Isaac[32] and to his son Jacob, whose name God later changed to Israel.[33] Undeniably, God has blessed the Jewish people abundantly, and He has blessed all families of the earth through them. After all, Jesus came through Abraham's line, and it is through Him alone that we can be saved from judgment. Now, many Jewish people reject Jesus Christ. Like all people who refuse God's mercy, these individuals will be judged. Yet, it is a testament to God's love that the Jewish people and the nation of Israel exist at all.

The story of the Jewish people is a story of human rebellion and the love of God. Time and time again, they have shown the rest of the world what it means to have a relationship with God. In summary, we've all walked away from God, but He doesn't wash His hands of us. God frequently warned the Jewish people they would be scattered around the globe if they rejected Him.[34] They didn't listen. In 70 A.D., the Romans destroyed the city of Jerusalem, taking the Jewish people into captivity. They were scattered all over the earth. Out of love, God judged their rebellion, disciplining them in the hope they would understand their need for Him.

While in these foreign lands, God also warned the Jewish people they would find nothing but persecution.[35] Although they would be persecuted, God promised to preserve their identity as Jewish people.[36] Well, for over 1,800 years, the Jewish people were scattered throughout the world. Everywhere they went they were persecuted, culminating in the Holocaust. In spite of the persecution, as promised, God preserved them. The Jewish people retained their unique identity. This is extraordinary. After all, how often do you run into a Moabite? When was the last time you saw a Hittite or an Ammonite? Museum mannequins don't count. No one can take a trip to the nations of Moab or Edom today, but amazingly, the nation of Israel is a common tourist destination.

Indeed, God preserved the Jewish people for a reason. At the appointed time, He promised to bring them back to their homeland.[37] In the early 20th century, as a result of World War I, control of modern-day Israel was transferred from the Ottoman Empire to Britain. The British issued the Balfour Declaration, announcing their intention to create a homeland for the Jewish people. This prepared modern-day Israel for Jewish settlement. After the Holocaust, the Jewish people were prepared to go back to the land of their ancestors. Shortly afterward, just as the Bible foretold, the nation of Israel was reborn in a single day.[38]

Still, the Jewish people aren't exactly going to win any popularity contests. They have been hated throughout history, and things definitely haven't changed with the re-establishment of Israel. Since God chose to reach out to the world through the Jewish people, they are hated. Of course, because of the revolt at Babel, God didn't have much of a choice. At Babel, the human race rebelled against His instructions. Due to their revolt, God confused their language and divided the families of the earth into nations.

All of these nations had rejected Him, so He couldn't possibly have reached out to the rest of the world through any of them. They wanted nothing to do with Him. Instead, God chose one faithful man out of the world to establish a new nation, through which all families of the earth would be blessed. While this blessing was fulfilled in Jesus, a physical descendant of Abraham and our Savior, the achievements of many Jewish people have also blessed the world richly.

Despite making up less than one percent of the world's population, the Jewish people have made numerous contributions to society. Albert Einstein, Joseph Pulitzer and Levi Strauss were all Jewish. Jonas Salk created the first polio vaccine. Gabriel Lippman discovered color photography. Chemist Fritz Haber and physicist Niels Bohr are just two of the many Jewish individuals who have received the Nobel Prize. Ralph Lauren and Calvin Klein are giants in fashion, while Estée Lauder was renowned in cosmetics. Michael Dell and Mark Zuckerberg are famous in the technology sector. Marcus Goldman, Henry Lehman and Jacob Schiff were extremely influential financiers. Steven Spielberg, Lorne Michaels and David Geffen are all well-known producers, and the number of Jewish entertainers is astoundingly large. Haym Solomon financed the Revolutionary War and visionary publisher Hank Greenspun was the real Forrest Gump. Without question, when God makes a promise, He keeps it.

Unsurprisingly, the success of the Jewish people has drawn a lot of jealousy through the years. Surely, God has blessed them to grab our attention, but for a much different reason. He chose a people group out of the earth, because of the faith of one man, to give the world a visible example of our nature and His nature. God's relationship with the Jewish people is a symbolic reminder of the relationship He has with everyone. In short, God loves us and we rebel against Him anyway. He blesses us out of His love, but usually, God's blessings just make us grow further from Him. He is the only reason for our success, but we think it's all about us. Naturally, our pride grows. We focus more on ourselves. We live by our own rules, and to get our attention, God disciplines us. He doesn't give up on us. He allows us to experience the consequences of our sins so that we focus less on ourselves and more on Him. We are disciplined to realize our need for Him. This is unpleasant, and we don't like it, but it is for our own good. Sadly, by and large, people rebel all the more.

For the overwhelming majority of the Jewish people, the great blessings they've been given and the persecutions they've endured have just hardened their hearts. God blessed and disciplined them so they would focus on His love for them and their need for Him. Yet, most Jewish people have rejected God. In so doing, they will be condemned to eternal separation from their Creator and His unending love. Likewise, most people reject God, and they are growing more vocal in their hatred of Him.

This is hardly unexpected. People aren't crucified for being politically correct. Before His death, Jesus said to His followers "If the world hate you, ye know that it hated me before it hated you."[39] In other words, you'll know you're in good company. He added "If they have persecuted me, they will also persecute you."[40] Without a doubt, the world hates Jesus Christ, and they take it out on Christians. The root of this hatred isn't hard to pinpoint. In a nutshell, people who reject God feel guilty for rebelling against Him, but they don't want to hear about it.[41] Naturally, these individuals try to justify their wrongdoing. They want everyone to legitimize their sinful behavior, because deep down, they know what they are doing is wrong. Christians don't fall in line with the plan, and rebellious human beings can't stand it.

Often, people lash out at Christians. For agreeing with God, followers of Christ are called insensitive, hateful or bigoted. Nothing could be further from the truth. Simply put, people think God is out to spoil their fun, but they misinterpret His love. They think He hates them, but God has nothing but love for everyone. Some people might say "But doesn't the Bible say God hates sinners?" Not at all! Sure, the Bible says God hates "all workers of iniquity,"[42] but the Hebrew word for hate also means "set against."[43] God is love.[44] His love is unconditional, because His very nature is love. The Bible says "God commendeth his love toward us, in that, while we were yet sinners, Christ died for us."[45] The Father loved the world so much He sent Jesus on a rescue mission. Jesus loved the world so much He voluntarily laid down His life to suffer the punishment we deserved for our sins.

On the other hand, hate implies a lack of caring for a person's well-being. Hatred is a desire to see someone hurt without anything good coming from it. Obviously, this isn't what God wants for anyone. Indeed, the Bible says God wants everyone to be saved.[46] Think of it this way. God created all of us in His image.[47] Well, sin is a deadly disease. God hates sin because it is destructive like any other disease. He has offered us the cure for our disease: Jesus. The problem? We don't think we need Jesus. Sin has corrupted our hearts and minds to the point where we don't even recognize we are sick. This upsets God. His wrath is on sinners.[48] The Bible says He is angry with the wicked every day.[49] Why is He angry? Simply put, He's mad people are rejecting the cure for their sin problem. His anger is out of love.

A good parent hates anything that hurts their children, because they love their children so much they want nothing bad to happen to them. Sin is destructive, and God doesn't grade on a curve. Everyone wants to shrug it off and say "nobody's perfect" when they do something wrong, but that's not how it works with God. He has a zero-tolerance policy toward sin. He is perfectly loving, so He will not condone sin of any kind. He is perfectly just, so He will not let any sinful behavior go unpunished.

Sin is deadly, and God hates it. He's angry when we sin, just like a parent is angry with their child when they do wrong. So, God sets Himself against people who sin without a care, just like any loving parent wouldn't accept their child rejecting the life-saving cure for their disease. You'd be mad if someone you loved refused life-saving treatment. You'd do whatever you could to change their mind. You would be set against them because of their decision to refuse what's best for them. You would try to influence them to get the cure. Without question, God does what He can to convince people Jesus is the way, the truth and the life, just like a parent would try anything to convince their child to take the life-saving cure. God lovingly draws all of us to the Cross.

Now, if God doesn't hate anyone, why does He sentence people who reject Jesus to Hell? Out of love for the rest of creation, God must condemn and punish evil. He must protect people from evil. As uncomfortable as it may sound, God lovingly respects a person's final decision to hate Him. He gives them what they want: eternal separation from Him. It's just like a parent allowing their child to reject life-saving treatment. Ultimately, love can't be forced. God will respect everybody's decision to reject Jesus, the cure for our deadly sin disease. Everyone in Hell has made up their mind, although God wished they had decided otherwise. He wanted better for them, but you can't force love.

Regardless, most people could care less. It's a sign of the times. After all, as it was in the days of Noah, so it will also be prior to the return of Jesus Christ.[50] These days, like it was before the floodwaters came, people mock the idea of judgment. Armed with the battle cry of 'you only live once,' they continue their rebellion against God without a care in the world. In reality, living for the moment isn't a good call. It doesn't matter if people agree with you or if your particular brand of sin is legalized. The opinions of other sinful human beings count for nothing. They are irrelevant. What God says, goes. Whether you want it to be true or not, every soul will exist forever, either in Heaven or Hell.

Overall, life comes down to a single choice. You might say "I'll take my chances," but why would you gamble on something so important? You may think this life is all there is, but what if you're wrong? Death comes to us all, and it can come without warning. Age isn't a factor. When you die, the fact remains, all that matters is whether you accepted or rejected Jesus Christ.

Still, you might think "This is good and all, but I don't want to give up what I'm doing now." Well, are the pleasures of this world worth a lifetime of loneliness and ever-present guilt, with Hell to look forward to when the party is over? Jesus said, "For what shall it profit a man, if he shall gain the whole world, and lose his own soul?"[51] Everything you try to keep in this life, you lose in the end. You can choose to keep living for yourself, but when your life is over, it'll be gone. Whoever wants to hang on to a life of sin will lose it, and eternity is a long time to be wrong.

You might object "Yeah, but Christians are just a bunch of hypocrites. They sin all the time." Don't blame professing Christians for your unbelief. Just because someone claims to be a Christian doesn't mean they are one. The Bible says all people must give an account to God,[52] and when that happens everybody's cards will be on the table. Besides, even true Christians sin every now and then. Christians aren't sinless by any means, but they do sin less over time. Most importantly, the sins of the Christian have been forgiven. The Bible says "the wages of sin is death; but the gift of God is eternal life through Jesus Christ our Lord."[53] The price for a life of sin is steep. Either you pay that price, or you can accept Jesus' full payment for your sin debt. It's one or the other.

Sadly, you may reject this gift because you think it isn't as important as other things in your life. You might say "I have things I need to do before I become a Christian." Nothing is more important than a person's relationship with God. To put Him off isn't a smart move. What if you die tonight? Indeed, not everyone has the opportunity to wait until their deathbed. Tomorrow isn't guaranteed and if you die before you become a Christian, you will be condemned to eternal torment without a second chance. Any person who rejects God will receive exactly what they want.

Hell is eternal separation from God. It isn't a metaphor or a state of mind. It's a real place. When people reject God, they make it clear they want nothing to do with Him. Since God won't force anyone to love Him, everyone who rejects Him will get their way. They will be completely separated from Him, but it isn't going to be like they imagined. To put it another way, Hell isn't a place where you're going to party with all of your friends.

On the contrary, no human experience can be compared to Hell. Sure, people say they had a 'hellish' day or they've 'been through Hell,' but the worst experiences in this life don't even come close to the real deal. Jesus described Hell as a place of never-ending conscious torment, "Where their worm dieth not, and the fire is not quenched."[54] In addition to undying maggots and unquenchable fire, Hell is also described as "the blackness of darkness for ever"[55] and a place where there will be "weeping and gnashing of teeth."[56] Typically, people will respond by saying eternal punishment is cruel, but cruelty would be a punishment that doesn't fit the crime. Surely, there is nothing excessive about Hell. Far from it, a sin against an infinite, eternal God deserves an infinite, eternal punishment.

Legally, the punishment for a crime depends on who the victim is. For example, there's a big difference between punching a homeless guy and hitting the President of the United States. Well, by definition, all sin is rebellion against God. Since God is infinite and eternal, a sin against Him merits an infinite, eternal punishment. This is why only

Jesus, the eternal, infinite and sinless Son of God, could pay the penalty for our sins in full. If we reject His full payment, we would have to pay off our own sin debt. We could never make that payment in full, because we can do nothing to take our own sin away. As a result, the punishment for our wrongdoing could never stop, because our guilt would always remain. For people who refuse the free gift of salvation, "the smoke of their torment ascendeth up for ever and ever: and they have no rest day nor night."[57] Hell lasts forever. It is a place of eternal torment for everyone who rejects Jesus Christ.

When it's all said and done, all that matters is having a personal relationship with God, but many people prefer religion. They would rather try to bribe God by doing nice things, because they don't want to address their sin problem. Of course, good deeds can't undo past sins, and justice will be served. Overall, people try to make it all about them, and not about God. They make it about their imagined ability, and they ignore God's character. They try to earn God's forgiveness by asking Him to look the other way while they keep rebelling. They expect going to church or reading the Bible will be enough to win over God, but He will not be bribed. Jesus said "Come unto me, all ye that labour and are heavy laden, and I will give you rest."[58] Doing a lot of good deeds won't get the job done. You must be born again.

Among non-Christians, and certain religious people who claim to follow Christ, the phrase 'born again' is code for a type of Christian who is to be avoided at all costs. In reality, to be a Christian, you must be born again. It may not be popular, but this is hardly a surprise. Jesus said, "wide is the gate, and broad is the way, that leadeth to destruction, and many there be which go in thereat."[59] He added that "narrow is the way, which leadeth unto life, and few there be that find it."[60] Trusting in Jesus Christ has never been the popular thing to do. If they were being honest, many non-Christians would readily admit they don't want you to be born again. It's no secret. Most people would rather live by their own rules. They throw away their soul on pleasures, possessions and a wild-goose chase for purpose, because they don't want God in their lives. Since they aren't punished right away, they think they'll get away with it, but they mistake God's loving patience for His approval. They refuse to acknowledge they'll be held accountable for their wrongdoing, but it doesn't change the fact they will be judged. Their guilty conscience confirms this, and they do whatever they can to suppress it.

As a result, everyone who is born again in Christ will be persecuted. People have an intense hatred of Jesus, because they fear He might be exactly who He claimed to be. In the back of their mind, they'll ask "What if I'm wrong?" Indeed, what if there is a place of eternal conscious torment for everyone who rejects Jesus? This rightly terrifies people, but instead of exploring the issue, they do anything in their power to shut Christians up. After all, Christians are another reminder of their guilt. They don't hate Hindus and no one has issues with Buddha. Nobody uses Allah as a curse word. None of these man-made religions deal with sin, so they don't attract the hatred of the world. Frankly, however, people who reject Jesus Christ have no power. What's the worst thing they can do? Jesus said "And fear not them which kill the body, but are not able to kill the soul: but rather fear him which is able to destroy both soul and body in hell."[61]

People commonly misplace their fears. They are afraid of what other individuals think or what pain they could cause in their lives, but they neglect their standing before God. The choice is yours. Jesus said, "I am the way, the truth, and the life: no man cometh unto the Father, but by me."[62] That's the reality of it, even if you don't want it to be that way. Beliefs don't change the truth. Jesus said "for this cause came I into the world, that I should bear witness unto the truth. Every one that is of the truth heareth my voice."[63] The world is full of lies, but they all stem from the same lie told way back in the Garden of Eden: "ye shall be as gods, knowing good and evil."[64] You've been lied to. We all have been. The question is, will you continue to believe the lie? Are the things of this world worth eternal regret, anger and unimaginable torment? It's either Jesus or the world, eternal life in Heaven or eternal torment in Hell.

Everybody who listens to the truth obeys the words of Jesus. The Lord Jesus said if you trust in Him, "ye shall know the truth, and the truth shall make you free."[65] To be set free from your sin debt, you must first repent. Repentance is a change of mind that results in a change of action. When you repent, you're changing your mind about how serious your sin problem is, and you take action by turning to God in faith to solve it. In other words, you confess the seriousness of your sin problem, and admit only Jesus is able to take care of this problem because of His death on the Cross.

If you truly change your mind and believe, it will result in a change of behavior. Through faith in Jesus Christ, you are born again by the Holy Spirit. You become a new creation. The Holy Spirit will enable you to turn from sin,[66] but you must change your mind and believe the good news of Jesus' death, burial and Resurrection.[67] Jesus stated "Not every one that saith unto me, Lord, Lord, shall enter into the kingdom of heaven; but he that doeth the will of my Father which is in heaven."[68] Only people who do the will of the Father go to Heaven. What's the will of the Father? Jesus explained "And this is the will of him that sent me, that every one which seeth the Son, and believeth on him, may have everlasting life: and I will raise him up at the last day."[69]

This is more than having faith that God exists. Believing in the existence of God is all well and good, but it won't take care of your sin problem. Leaning on God only when you need something won't do either. He isn't a genie. To be right with God, you must trust in Jesus Christ alone for the forgiveness of your sins. When you truly repent and trust in Jesus, you will be born again. The Holy Spirit will come to live within you,[70] and He will change your sinful ways.

This doesn't mean you will stop sinning, but you will want to sin less and less. When you do sin, the Holy Spirit will convict you. Put differently, you will feel guilty when you do wrong. The Holy Spirit will gently remind you of your sin, and make you able to turn from it. The Holy Spirit fills us with love, joy, patience, kindness, goodness, faithfulness, gentility and discipline.[71] He heals our guilt, our shame and our emptiness. He is the guarantee of our salvation and our Comforter in all things.[72] In other words, you become a new creation. You are declared not guilty based upon what Jesus did, and you are credited with His perfect righteousness.[73] God looks at you and sees the sinless life of Jesus. By faith in Christ, you won't be judged for your sin and you will be rewarded with eternal life.[74]

So, why are we here? Simply put, we're here to have a personal relationship with God. To enter into a relationship with Him, you must place your trust in Jesus Christ for the forgiveness of your sins. If you have believed, confess your faith in Jesus by crying out to Him in prayer. If you've never prayed before or you're not sure what to say, there is a suggested prayer below. It doesn't have to be exact. There are no "magic" words you must recite. For that matter, any prayer is empty if you don't mean it. God sees the heart. It is not a prayer that saves you; it is the faith in your heart.

> Father, I'm a helpless sinner. There's nothing I can do to earn Your forgiveness, and I can't change on my own. Have mercy on me. I put my trust in Your Son Jesus as my Lord and Savior. I believe His death is the full payment for my sins. Please forgive me of every sin I have ever committed. Cleanse my heart Lord. I will no longer live for myself. I pray the Holy Spirit turns me from my sinful ways. Help me live in a way that glorifies You alone. In Jesus' name I pray, Amen.

References

Preface

[1] Romans 1:20.
[2] John 14:6.
[3] Matthew 5:48.
[4] Isaiah 53:5.

The Why Generation

[1] Genesis 1:1.
[2] Genesis 1:31.
[3] Genesis 1:29-30.
[4] Genesis 2:17.
[5] Genesis 3:19. See also Romans 5:12.
[6] Romans 3:23.
[7] 2 Thessalonians 1:9.
[8] John 3:16.
[9] Philippians 2:5-11. See also Isaiah 9:6; John 1:1-3 and Colossians 2:9.
[10] 1 Peter 2:24.
[11] Acts 2:24.
[12] John 3:36 and John 6:40.

Living in a Material World

[1] Gould, S., *Natural History* **103**(2):14, 1994.
[2] See Psalm 90:2; Isaiah 57:15; Deuteronomy 33:27 and 1 Timothy 1:17.
[3] Davies, P., *New Scientist* **179**:32, 12 July, 2003.
[4] Slack, G., What neo-creationists get right—an evolutionist shares lessons he's learned from the Intelligent Design camp, *The Scientist*, <http://www.thescientist.com/templates/trackable/display/news.jsp?type=news&o_url=news/display/54759&id=54759, 20 June 2008>.
[5] Dawkins, R., *The Blind Watchmaker*, W.W. Norton, New York, p. 115, 1986.
[6] Popper, K.R., Scientific Reduction and the Essential Incompleteness of All Science; in Ayala, F. and Dobzhansky, T., Eds., *Studies in the Philosophy of Biology*, University of California Press, Berkeley, p. 270, 1974.
[7] Gitt, W., *In the Beginning Was Information*, 3rd English ed., Christliche Literatur-Verbreitung, Bielefeld, Germany, 2001. Gitt, W., *Am Anfang war die Information*, 3. überarbeitete und erweiterte Auflage, Hänssler Verlag, Holzgerlingen, 2002. The definitions for the laws of nature about information are taken from former director and professor at the German Federal Institute of Physics and Technology, Dr. Werner Gitt. He was the head of the Department of Information Technology. The ten laws of nature about information are largely discussed on pages 131 through 150 of his book, *In the Beginning Was Information.*

[8] *Encyclopaedia Britannica* **1:**666, 1992. See also the *Routledge Encyclopedia of Philosophy*.
[9] Lewis, C.S, *The Business of Heaven*, Fount Paperbacks, U.K., p. 97, 1984.
[10] Haldane, J.B.S. *Possible Worlds*, p. 209; cited in Lewis, C.S., *Miracles*, Fontana, London, p. 19, 1960 (first published 1947).
[11] Provine, W.B., *Origins Research* **16**(1), p.9, 1994.
[12] Exodus 20:16. See also Leviticus 19:11 and Proverbs 6:16-19.
[13] Matthew 5:44; Luke 6:27.
[14] The Dalai Lama, *The Universe in a Single Atom*, Broadway Books, New York, 2005, p. 107.
[15] Colossians 1:16.
[16] Jesus spoke of the good angels in Matthew 22:30 as "the angels of God in heaven" and the bad angels in Matthew 25:41 as "the devil and his angels."
[17] Hebrews 1:14.
[18] See Joshua 5:13-14; Matthew 28:2-7; Luke 24:4-6, John 20:12-13 & Acts 12:7-10.
[19] Hebrews 13:2.
[20] See 2 Thessalonians 1:7 & 2 Peter 2:11.
[21] See Colossians 2:18; Revelation 19:10 & Romans 1:25.
[22] See Isaiah 14:13-14; Ezekiel 28:15 & 1 Timothy 3:6. Satan's rebellion is symbolically described in Isaiah 14:12-15 and Ezekiel 28:11-18. These two passages focus on the kings of Babylon and Tyre, respectively, but they also emphasize the spiritual power behind the throne. That spiritual power, of course, is supplied by none other than Satan. For example, Isaiah 14:12 describes the 'morning star' being cast out of Heaven. Surely, this didn't happen to the King of Babylon. Satan being cast down to earth is also consistent with Luke 10:18, which records Jesus saying "I beheld Satan as lightning fall from heaven." Likewise, Ezekiel 28:11-19 describes much more than a human king. The King of Tyre couldn't have possibly been in the Garden of Eden (Ezekiel 28:13) or a cherub (Ezekiel 28:14), which is a kind of angel. Incidentally, there are several kinds of angels, including cherubim, seraphim (Isaiah 6:2, 6) and archangels (Daniel 10:20-21). They also appear to be different in rank (Ephesians 6:12). That said, Isaiah 14:12-15 and Ezekiel 28:11-18 are clearly symbolic descriptions of Satan's failed rebellion against God.
[23] Revelation 12:3-4, 9.
[24] See Luke 10:18 & Isaiah 14:12.
[25] 2 Corinthians 4:4.
[26] Genesis 3:1-5.
[27] Genesis 3:4.
[28] Genesis 3:5.
[29] See Job 1:7-10 & Luke 22:31-32.
[30] Acts 10:34.
[31] Colossians 2:15 & 1 John 3:8.
[32] Matthew 25:41 & Revelation 20:10.
[33] 1 Peter 5:8.
[34] 2 Corinthians 11:14.
[35] See Leviticus 19:26, 31; Leviticus 20:6 & Deuteronomy 18:9-14.
[36] This section heavily relies upon *Alien Intrusion: UFOs and the Evolution Connection* by Gary Bates, published by Creation Book Publishers, Powder Springs, GA, 2011 (Sixth printing).

[37] Psalm 19:1.
[38] Hynek, J. and Vallée J., *The Edge of Reality: A Progress Report on Unidentified Flying Objects*, Chicago, IL, Henry Regnery Company, 1975, p. xii-xiii.
[39] Keel, J., *Our Haunted Planet*, Lakeville, MN, Galde Press, Inc., 2002, p. 89.
[40] Keel, J., *Operation Trojan Horse,* Lilburn, GA, Illuminet Press, 1996, p. 266.
[41] Ibid, p. 192.
[42] NOVA Online/Kidnapped by UFOs/John Mack (Interview with John Mack) <http://www.pbs.org/wgbh/nova/aliens/johnmack.html>.
[43] For a few examples see Daniel 4:13-17; Zechariah 1:9-11 and Acts 10:3.
[44] See Matthew 1:20 and Matthew 2:13.
[45] Acts 12:5-19.
[46] John 8:44.
[47] Vallée, J., *Confrontations*, New York, NY, Ballantine Books, 1990, p. 13.
[48] "Alien 'abductees' show real symptoms," <http://news.bbc.co.uk/2/hi/in_depth/sci_tech/2003/denver_2003/2769875.stm>, February 18, 2003.
[49] Quoted in Bates, G., *Alien Intrusion: UFOs and the Evolution Connection,* Powder Springs, GA, Creation Book Publishers, 2011, p. 257.
[50] Ibid, p. 259
[51] Strieber, W., *Transformation: The Breakthrough*, New York, NY, Avon Books, 1997, p. 172.
[52] Ankerberg, J. & Weldon, J., *The Facts on UFOs and Other Supernatural Phenomena*, Eugene, OR, Harvest House, 1992, p. 13.
[53] 1 Timothy 4:1.
[54] Ruse, M., "How evolution became a religion: creationists correct?" *National Post,* May 13, 2000, pp. B1, B3, B7.
[55] Nagel, T., *The Last Word*, Oxford University Press, New York, 1997, p. 130.
[56] Huxley, A., *Ends and Means: An Inquiry into the Nature of Ideals and into the Methods Employed for Their Realization*, 1937, p. 270.
[57] Dahmer, Jeffrey, in an interview with Stone Phillips, *Dateline* NBC, Nov. 29, 1994.
[58] Matthew 13:42.

The Gospel Truth

[1] 2 Timothy 3:16. See also 2 Peter 1:21.
Note: This section is heavily influenced by Edwards, B., *Nothing But the Truth*, Darlington, UK: Evangelical Press, 2006, pp.116-143 and Geisler, N.L. and Nix, W.E., *A General Introduction to the Bible,* Chicago: Moody Press, 1986.
[2] Bruce, F. F. *The New Testament Documents: Are They Reliable?*, Downer's Grove, IL: InterVarsity Press, 1971, p. 15.
[3] Geisler, N., *Christian Apologetics*, Grand Rapids: Baker Book House, 1976, p. 307. See also Mcdowell, J., and Wilson, B., *A Ready Defense*, Nashville, TN: Thomas Nelson Publishers, 1993, pp. 42-55; Slick, M., "Manuscript evidence for superior New Testament reliability" <carm.org/manuscript-evidence> and Sarfati, J., "Should we trust the Bible?" <creation.com/trust-the-bible>.
[4] Pinnock, C., *Biblical Revelation: The Foundation of Christian Theology*, Chicago: Moody Press, 1971, pp. 238-39, 365-66. See also France, R. T. *The Evidence for*

Jesus. Downers Grove: IVP, 1986, pp. 135-136 and Slick, M., "Manuscript evidence for superior New Testament reliability" <http://carm.org/manuscript-evidence>.
[5] Carson, D.A., *The King James Version Debate*, Grand Rapids: Baker Book House, 1979, p. 56.
[6] Edwards, B., "Chapter 17: Why 66?" <answersingenesis.org/articles/nab2/why-sixty-six> of Ham, K., et al., *New Answers Book 2,* Green Forest, AR: Master Books, 2008, pp. 147-156. See also Edwards, B., "Why 66: How can we be sure which books belong in the Bible?" <answersingenesis.org/articles/am/v2/n4/why-66>.
[7] Hebrews 6:18.
[8] Jeremiah 17:9.
[9] Genesis 8:21.
[10] Ecclesiastes 7:20.
[11] 2 Samuel 11.
[12] Acts 8:1-5; Acts 9:1-2; Galatians 1:13; 1 Corinthians 15:9. Note: Paul was also known as Saul.
[13] Genesis 27.
[14] Exodus 2:11-15.
[15] Psalm 22:16.
[16] Zechariah 13:6.
[17] Luke 23:33.
[18] Old Testament predicted: Micah 5:2. New Testament fulfilled: Matthew 2:1; Luke 2:1-7.
[19] Old Testament predicted: Genesis 3:15; Isaiah 7:14. New Testament fulfilled: Matthew 1:18-24; Luke 1:34-35.
[20] Old Testament predicted: Psalm 72:10-11. New Testament fulfilled: Matthew 2:11.
[21] Old Testament predicted: Isaiah 40:3; Malachi 3:1. New Testament fulfilled: Matthew 3:1-3; Matthew 11:7-14.
[22] Old Testament predicted: Psalm 78:2; Isaiah 6:9. New Testament fulfilled: Matthew 13:34-35; Matthew 13:10-16.
[23] Old Testament predicted: Psalm 69:4. New Testament fulfilled: John 15:24-25.
[24] Old Testament predicted: Isaiah 53:4-5. New Testament fulfilled: Matthew 8:16-17; Matthew 12:15-21.
[25] Old Testament predicted: Zechariah 9:9. New Testament fulfilled: John 12:12-15.
[26] Old Testament predicted: Psalm 41:9. New Testament fulfilled: John 13:18-27.
[27] Old Testament predicted: Zechariah 11:12. New Testament fulfilled: Matthew 26:14-15.
[28] Old Testament predicted: Isaiah 50:6. New Testament fulfilled: Matthew 27:30.
[29] Old Testament predicted: Isaiah 50:6. New Testament fulfilled: Matthew 26:67.
[30] Old Testament predicted: Psalm 69:19; Psalm 22:6-18; Isaiah 50:6. New Testament fulfilled: Mark 15:17-19.
[31] Old Testament predicted: Isaiah 53:9. New Testament fulfilled: Matthew 27:57-60; Luke 23:50-53; John 19:38-41.
[32] Old Testament predicted: Psalm 22:18. New Testament fulfilled: John 19:23-24.
[33] Old Testament predicted: Zechariah 12:10. New Testament fulfilled: John 19:34.
[34] Old Testament predicted: Psalm 34:20. New Testament fulfilled: John 19:32-33.
[35] Old Testament predicted: Psalm 16:10; Isaiah 53:10-11. New Testament fulfilled: Mark 16:6; Matthew 28:5-7.

[36] Old Testament predicted: Isaiah 66:8. Fulfilled: May 14th, 1948 with Israel's formal declaration of independence.
[37] Wilson, C., *Rocks, Relics and Biblical Reliability,* Grand Rapids, MI: Zondervan, 1977, p. 126.
[38] Albright, W., *The Archaeology of Palestine*, rev. edition, Harmondsworth, Middlesex: Pelican Books, 1960, pp.127-128.
[39] Schoville, Keith., *Biblical Archaeology in Focus*, Grand Rapids, MI: Baker, 1978, p. 156.
[40] Geisler, N., and Holden, J., *The Popular Handbook of Archaeology and the Bible.* Eugene, OR: Harvest House, 2012.
[41] Ecclesiastes 1:6.
[42] Job 14:18-19.
[43] Ecclesiastes 1:7; Isaiah 55:10.
[44] Psalm 135:7; Jeremiah 10:13.
[45] Job 38:16.
[46] Leviticus 17:11.
[47] Psalm 8:8.
[48] Genesis 1:11; Genesis 1:21; Genesis 1:25.
[49] Leviticus 13:1-14:57; Numbers 5:2-4; Deuteronomy 23:10.
[50] Deuteronomy 23:12-14; Leviticus 13:47-58.
[51] Numbers 19:11-22; Leviticus 11:24-28.
[52] Leviticus 15.
[53] Genesis 1:1.
[54] Genesis 1:3.
[55] Genesis 1:5.
[56] Genesis 1:6-8.
[57] Genesis 1:9-12.
[58] Genesis 1:14-18.
[59] Genesis 1:20-22.
[60] Genesis 1:24-30.
[61] Genesis 2:7; 2:19.
[62] Genesis 2:20.
[63] Genesis 2:19.
[64] Grigg, R., Naming the animals: all in a day's work for Adam, *Creation* **18**(4):46–49, 1996.
[65] Genesis 2:21.
[66] Genesis 1:31.
[67] Genesis 1:29.
[68] Genesis 2:2-3.
[69] Genesis 1:5; Genesis 1:8; Genesis 1:13; Genesis 1:19; Genesis 1:23; Genesis 1:31.
[70] Exodus 20:11.
[71] This illustration can be likened to all radiometric (radio-isotopic) dating methods.
[72] For more on radiometric dating methods consult Batten, D. (Ed.), Catchpoole, D., Sarfati, J. and Wieland, C., Chapter 4, What about Carbon Dating? *The Creation Answers Book*, Creation Book Publishers, 2006.
[73] Austin, S. A. 1986. Mt. St. Helens and Catastrophism. *Acts & Facts*. 15 (7).
[74] Genesis 6-9.
[75] Genesis 7:11 and Genesis 8:2.

[76] See Williams, E.L., Providence Canyon, Stewart County, Georgia—Evidence of recent rapid erosion, *Creation Research Society Quarterly* **32**(1):29–43, 1995 and Gibson, R., Canyon Creation, *Creation* **22**(4):46–48, September 2000.
[77] Morris, J. 2001. How Long Does It Take for a Canyon to Form? *Acts & Facts*. 30 (12).
[78] Yeoman, B., Schweitzer's Dangerous Discovery, *Discover* **27**(4):37–41, 77, 2006.
[79] Job 40:15-24.
[80] The word 'dragon' appears, as a reference to a literal animal, in many verses from the 1599 Geneva Bible and the King James Version of the Bible (1611). Here are a few examples: Psalm 74:13; Psalm 91:13; Isaiah 13:22; Isaiah 34:13; Jeremiah 9:11 and Jeremiah 10:22.
[81] The following sources are worth consulting for scientific observations consistent with a young earth: Humphreys, R., Evidence for a young world, *Impact* **384**, June 2005; Batten, D. (Ed.), Catchpoole, D., Sarfati, J. and Wieland, C., Chapter 4, What about Carbon Dating? *The Creation Answers Book*, Creation Book Publishers, 2006, pp. 80-86; Sarfati, J., Chapter 11, Science and the Young Earth, *Refuting Compromise*, Green Forest, AR: Master Books, 2004. See also Batten, D., "Age of the earth: 101 evidences for a young age of the earth and the universe," <creation.com/age-of-the-earth>.
[82] See Cherfas, J., Ancient DNA: still busy after death, *Science* **253**:1354–1356, 20 September 1991; Cano, R. J., H. N. Poinar, N. J. Pieniazek, A. Acra, and G. O. Poinar, Jr. Amplification and sequencing of DNA from a 120-135-million-year-old weevil, *Nature* **363**:536–8, 10 June 1993; Krings, M., A. Stone, R. W. Schmitz, H. Krainitzki, M. Stoneking, and S. Pääbo, Neandertal DNA sequences and the origin of modern humans, *Cell* **90**:19–30, July 11, 1997; Lindahl, T, Unlocking nature's ancient secrets, *Nature* **413**:358–359, 27 September 2001; Vreeland, R. H.,W. D. Rosenzweig, and D. W. Powers, Isolation of a 250 million-year-old halotolerant bacterium from a primary salt crystal, *Nature* **407**:897–900, 19 October 2000. Sources taken from Humphreys, R., Evidence for a young world, *Impact* **384**, June 2005.
[83] For some information on the chemistry of DNA, and its inability to last millions of years in natural environments, consult Lindahl, T., Instability and decay of the primary structure of DNA, *Nature* **362**(6422):709–715, 1993 and Pääbo, S., Ancient DNA, *Scientific American* **269**(5):60–66, 1993.
[84] Sanford, J., *Genetic Entropy and the Mystery of the Genome*, Ivan Press, 2005.
[85] See Sarfati, J., The Earth's Magnetic Field: Evidence That the Earth is Young, *Creation* **20**(2):15-19, 1998, <creation.com/magfield> and Humphreys, R., Earth's magnetic field is decaying steadily—with a little rhythm, *CRSQ* **47**(3):193–201; 2011.
[86] See Humphreys, R., Evidence for a young world, *Impact* **384**, June 2005 and Sarfati, J., Chapter 11, Science and the Young Earth, *Refuting Compromise*, Green Forest, AR: Master Books, 2004, pp. 345-348.
[87] Genesis 2:16-17.
[88] Since angels are created beings, they are bound by time. In other words, they had a beginning in time. This means they had to be created, at the earliest, on the first day of creation (Genesis 1:1). In Job 38:4, God asks a man named Job, "Where wast thou when I laid the foundations of the earth?" In Job 34:7, we find out that the angels, called the "sons of God" in the verse, saw God lay the foundations of the earth. This could be a reference to the first day of creation, when God made the earth (Genesis 1:1), or it could be a reference to when God made the dry land appear on the third day

of creation (Genesis 1:9-10, 13). So, we can conclude angels were created no later than the third day of creation. Since God called the sixth day of creation very good (Genesis 1:31), and He blessed the seventh day (Genesis 2:3), this means Satan rebelled sometime shortly after the week of creation. Why shortly? Well, Adam and Eve were commanded to "Be fruitful, and multiply" (Genesis 1:28). Given that they hadn't sinned yet, they would've heartily obeyed. With their physically perfect bodies, Eve would've probably conceived within her first menstrual cycle. As a result, their rebellion against God likely occurred less than a month after the week of creation. Obviously, Satan rebelled before Adam and Eve. So, we can conclude Satan rebelled shortly after the week of creation.

[89] Genesis 3:1.

[90] Genesis 3:4.

[91] Genesis 3:5.

[92] See Genesis 3:19; Romans 8:20–22.

[93] Romans 3:23.

[94] Genesis 3:15.

[95] Genesis 4:1-12, 17.

[96] Genesis 5:4.

[97] Leviticus 18-20.

[98] Genesis 6:5-8.

[99] Genesis 6:11-22.

[100] Genesis 6:19-20; Genesis 7:1-10. Now, you might be wondering, "What's the deal with this 'seven pairs' business? I thought only one pair of each animal went on the Ark?" Well, Genesis 7:2-3 says the following: "Of every clean beast thou shalt take to thee by sevens, the male and his female: and of beasts that are not clean by two, the male and his female. Of fowls also of the air by sevens, the male and the female; to keep seed alive upon the face of all the earth." There is some debate about whether this passage is referring to seven or seven pairs of each kind of clean beast and bird. We'll go with seven pairs because modern translators seem to favor it. That said, what were clean animals? They are defined in Leviticus 11 and Deuteronomy 14. Although it may seem weird for something recorded in Leviticus and Deuteronomy to clarify something in Genesis, Moses did put together Genesis, Leviticus and Deuteronomy. For the record, there weren't many clean animals listed in Leviticus and Deuteronomy, so room on the Ark wouldn't have been an issue. At this, some people wonder if there is a contradiction between Genesis 6:19-20 and Genesis 7:2-3. Not at all! Genesis 6:19-20 records God instructing Noah to preserve two of every kind of animal. In Genesis 7:2-3, God gives additional information. Obviously, since there were seven pairs of clean animals on the Ark, there was also a pair of clean animals on the Ark. After all, you can't have seven pairs without first having one pair. So, there's no contradiction. Yet, why did God have Noah bring the extra clean animals? Simply put, they were for sacrifice. Indeed, after his stay on the Ark, Noah built "an altar unto the Lord; and took of every clean beast, and of every clean fowl, and offered burnt offerings on the altar" (Genesis 8:20).

[101] This section is heavily influenced by Batten, D. (Ed.), Catchpoole, D., Sarfati, J. and Wieland, C., Chapter 13, How did the animals fit on Noah's Ark? *The Creation Answers Book*, Creation Book Publishers, 2006 and Woodmorappe, J., *Noah's Ark: A Feasibility Study*, Institute for Creation Research. El Cajon, CA, USA, 1997.

[102] Genesis 7:15, 21.

[103] Genesis 6:20, Genesis 7:8-9.
[104] Genesis 6:15. The ark was 300 cubits long, 50 cubits wide and 30 cubits high. Most people believe the cubit of the ark was around 18 inches, though cubits in ancient Near Eastern cultures range from roughly 17.5 inches to 22 inches.
[105] Genesis 6:14.
[106] Genesis 6:21.
[107] See Erickson, G. *et al.*, Dinosaurian growth patterns and rapid avian growth rates, *Nature* **412**(6845):429–433, 26 July 2001.
[108] Genesis 7:11; Genesis 8:13-14.
[109] A time of 70 years comes from the chronological information in Genesis. In Genesis 6:14-18, God told Noah to build an ark for him, his three sons and their wives. Noah had three sons, and they were old enough to be married. We learn in Genesis 5:32 that Noah was 500 when his first son Japheth was born. When the floodwaters came, Noah was 600, which we find out by reading Genesis 7:6. If 30 years are allowed for Noah's sons to be old enough to marry, this gives Noah and his sons 70 years to build the ark. The time is approximate, because it changes depending on when Noah's sons were married. A range of 55 to 75 years to complete the ark is plausible.
[110] Genesis 7:11.
[111] L. Bergeron, Deep waters, *New Scientist* **155**(2097):22–26, 1997. See also Harder, B., "Inner Earth May Hold More Water than the Seas," *National Geographic*, March 7, 2002, <http://news.nationalgeographic.com/news/2002/03/0307_0307_waterworld.html>; Than, K., "Huge 'Ocean' Discovered Inside Earth," *LiveScience*, February 28, 2007, <http://www.livescience.com/1312-huge-ocean-discovered-earth.html> and Harder, B., "Earth Contains a Vast Amount of Water, But Scientists Are Unsure of Its Origins," *Washington Post*, November 8, 2010, <http://www.washingtonpost.com/wp-dyn/content/article/2010/11/08/AR2010110804478.html>.
[112] The earth was formed out of water: Genesis 1:2; 2 Peter 3:5-6. God made dry land appear on the third day of creation: Genesis 1:9-10.
[113] See Nelson, B., *The Deluge Story in Stone*, Appendix 11, Flood Traditions, Figure 38, Augsburg, Minneapolis, 1931.
[114] For more information on the post-Flood Ice Age, consult Oard, M., *Frozen in Time*, Green Forest, AR: Master Books, 2004.
[115] 2 Peter 2:5.
[116] Genesis 9:1.
[117] Genesis 11:4.
[118] Ethnologue, a company that provides statistics on world languages, estimates 136 languages families exist according to their most recent research at the time of this publication. This number is likely to fluctuate as research continues. See Ethnologue, "Statistical Summaries," <www.ethnologue.com/ethno_docs/distribution.asp?by=family> from Lewis, M. Paul, Gary F. Simons, and Charles D. Fennig (eds.). 2013. *Ethnologue: Languages of the World, Seventeenth edition.* Dallas, Texas: SIL International. Online version: <http://www.ethnologue.com>.
[119] Dawkins, R. *Unweaving the Rainbow*, Boston, MA: Houghton-Miflin Co., 1998, p. 295.

[120] Gutin, J.C. "End of the Rainbow." *Discover*, November, 1994, pp. 71-75.
[121] Acts 17:26.
[122] Gould, S. *Ontogeny and Phylogeny*, Belknap-Harvard Press, 1977, pp. 127–128.
[123] Romans 3:23-24; Ephesians 2:8-9.
[124] Genesis 1:26.
[125] John 1:1.
[126] John 1:3.
[127] Colossians 1:17. See also Hebrews 1:3.
[128] Genesis 1:2.
[129] Matthew 3:16–17.
[130] Matthew 28:19.
[131] John 8:12.
[132] Colossians 1:15.
[133] Colossians 2:9.
[134] 2 Corinthians 4:6.
[135] Isaiah 43:11.
[136] Acts 16:31.
[137] Acts 16:34.
[138] Titus 2:13.
[139] Exodus 34:14; Deuteronomy 6:13; Matthew 4:10.
[140] John 20:28.
[141] Hebrews 4:15. See also 2 Corinthians 5:21 and Hebrews 7:26.
[142] John 3:16.
[143] Matthew 27:57-60; Luke 23:50-53; John 19:38-41.
[144] Isaiah 53:9.
[145] Matthew 16:21; John 2:18-22 and John 10:17-18. See also Matthew 12:39-40 and Matthew 27:62-64.
[146] Matthew 27:62-66.
[147] Matthew 27:65-66.
[148] Matthew 28:6-7; Mark 16:6; Luke 24:34. See also Romans 1:4; Romans 10:9; 1 Corinthians 15:2-4; 2 Timothy 2:8; 1 Peter 1:3-4.
[149] Matthew 28:1-6; Mark 16:1-7; Luke 24:1-12 and John 20:1-12.
[150] Acts 1:3.
[151] 1 Corinthians 15:5-8.
[152] Luke 24:36; John 20:26-29; John 21:1 and Acts 1:3-11.
[153] 1 Corinthians 15:6.
[154] Luke 24:37.
[155] Luke 24:38-40.
[156] Luke 24:41-45.
[157] Luke 22:44.
[158] Matthew 26:67-68; Mark 14:65 and Luke 22:63-64.
[159] Matthew 27:26 and Mark 15:15.
[160] Matthew 27:29.
[161] Matthew 27:30.
[162] John 19:31.
[163] John 19:32.
[164] John 19:33.
[165] See Psalm 34:20 for the prediction and John 19:36 for the recorded fulfillment.

[166] John 19:34.
[167] Matthew 28:11–15.
[168] Matthew 28:13.
[169] John 20:19.
[170] Mark 9:30-32.
[171] Luke 24:13-17.
[172] See Acts 4:1-12 and Acts 7:1-58.
[173] Matthew 26:69–75.
[174] See Acts 2:14-41 and Acts 3:11-26.
[175] Acts 4:1-12.
[176] Acts 7:1-57.
[177] Acts 7:57-58.
[178] Acts 7:58.
[179] Acts 8:3; Acts 22:4 and Galatians 1:13.
[180] Acts 9:1-9.
[181] John 20:25.
[182] John 20:27.
[183] John 20:28.
[184] Acts 2:24 and Acts 3:15.
[185] Revelation 21:1. See also Isaiah 65:17 and 2 Peter 3:13.
[186] Revelation 21:4.
[187] Lewis, C.S., *The Problem of Pain.* New York: Macmillan Publishing Company, 1962, p. 93.
[188] Genesis 3:1.
[189] Matthew 7:15.

Wolves in Sheep's Clothing

* All quotations from the Koran are taken from Abdullah Yusuf Ali's 1935 translation of the Koran into English.
[1] See Koran 2:40-42, 136, 285; Koran 3:3; Koran 4:47, 136, 163; Koran 10:37; Koran 21:7 and Koran 35:31.
[2] Koran 3:3.
[3] Koran 2:136.
[4] Koran 6:115. See also Koran 6:34; Koran 10:64 and Koran 18:27.
[5] Koran 15:90.
[6] Koran 15:91.
[7] Koran 6:34.
[8] Koran 2:106.
[9] Koran 4:82.
[10] Koran 16:101.
[11] Koran 2:256.
[12] Koran 8:12.
[13] Koran 9:29.
[14] Koran 29:46.
[15] Koran 4:171 and Koran 112:2-3.

[16] See Isaiah 9:6-7; John 1:1-3; John 10:30; John 20:28; Colossians 2:9; Titus 2:13; Hebrews 1:3; Hebrews 1:8; and 2 Peter 2:1.
[17] Koran 16:20-21 and Koran 25:3.
[18] Koran 22:73.
[19] Koran 3:49.
[20] Koran 5:110.
[21] Koran 37:125.
[22] See John 14:7-9 and John 17:3.
[23] See 2 Corinthians 4:6 and Colossians 2:9.
[24] Koran 112:1-4.
[25] See Koran 4:171 and Koran 112:1-4.
[26] See Koran 11:90 and Koran 85:14.
[27] 1 John 4:8. See also Romans 5:8; Ephesians 2:4; 1 John 4:10 and 1 John 4:16.
[28] 1 John 4:19.
[29] Koran 4:40.
[30] Koran 4:110.
[31] Koran 23:102-103. See also Koran 101:6-9.
[32] Koran 46:9. See also Koran 31:34.
[33] Koran 10:54.
[34] Koran 4:157.
[35] Koran 14:4.
[36] Koran 19:33.
[37] Koran 4:157-158. See also Koran 3:55.
[38] Koran 10:94. See also Koran 21:7.
[39] See Matthew 17:22-23 and John 10:15-18.
[40] See Mark 16:6-8; Matthew 28:5-7 and Acts 2:24.
[41] Koran 17:90-96 and Koran 29:50-52.
[42] See Koran 2:252-253; Koran 3:49 and Koran 5:110.
[43] Koran 36:78-79.
[44] Koran 5:110.
[45] See Koran 40:55; Koran 47:19 and Koran 48:2.
[46] Koran 46:9.
[47] Koran 19:17-19.
[48] Koran 4:158.
[49] See Koran 2:40-42, 136, 285; Koran 3:3; Koran 4:47, 136, 163; Koran 10:37; Koran 21:7 and Koran 35:31.
[50] See Koran 6:115; Koran 6:34; Koran 10:64 and Koran 18:27.
[51] John 14:6.
[52] *The Hadith According to Al Bukhari*, vol. 9:57. The Hadith records the sayings and deeds of Muhammad. Next to the Koran, it is the most important book in Islam.
[53] Matthew 5:12.
[54] John 10:30.
[55] John 10:33.
[56] 1 Timothy 3:16.
[57] John 20:28.
[58] John 20:29.
[59] John 14:28.
[60] John 5:19.

[61] John 21:17. See also John 16:30.
[62] Mark 13:32.
[63] Colossians 1:15.
[64] Colossians 1:16.
[65] John 14:9.
[66] John 5:18.
[67] John 19:7.
[68] See McConkie, B., *Mormon Doctrine*, Salt Lake City: Bookcraft, 1991, p. 163 and Hunter, M., *The Gospel Through the Ages*, Salt Lake City: Deseret Book Company, 1945, p. 15.
[69] See McConkie, B., *Mormon Doctrine*, Salt Lake City: Bookcraft, 1991, p. 163, pp. 576-577 and Smith, J., *Teachings of the Prophet Joseph Smith*, Salt Lake City: Deseret Book Company, 1976, p. 349, pp. 370-372.
[70] McConkie, B., *Mormon Doctrine*, Salt Lake City: Bookcraft, 1991, p. 516.
[71] McConkie, B., *Mormon Doctrine*, Salt Lake City: Bookcraft, 1991, p. 321. See also Smith, J., *Times and Seasons*, Vol. 5, pp. 613-614.
[72] Smith, J., *Teachings of the Prophet Joseph Smith*, Salt Lake City: Deseret Book Company, 1976, pp. 345-347, 354.
[73] See Deuteronomy 6:4; Deuteronomy 32:39; Psalm 86:10; Isaiah 43:10; Isaiah 44:6-8; Isaiah 45:5; Romans 3:29-30; 1 Corinthians 8:4; Galatians 3:20; 1 Thessalonians 1:9; 1 Timothy 1:17; James 2:19 and Jude 1:25.
[74] Isaiah 43:10.
[75] Alma 11:26-29.
[76] Smith, J., *Teachings of the Prophet Joseph Smith*, Salt Lake City: Deseret Book Company, 1976, pp. 345
[77] Psalm 90:2.
[78] Moroni 8:18.
[79] Isaiah 9:6-7; John 1:1-3; John 10:30; John 20:28; Colossians 2:9; Titus 2:13; Hebrews 1:3; Hebrews 1:8; and 2 Peter 2:1.
[80] John 1:3.
[81] See *The Watchtower*, May 15, 1963, p. 307; *The New World*, 284.
[82] Jehovah's Witnesses have their own 'Bible,' called the *New World Translation of the Holy Scriptures*.
[83] John 1:3.
[84] Hebrews 1:3.
[85] The following verses mention Michael the Archangel: Daniel 10:13; Daniel 10:21; Daniel 12:1; Jude 1:9 & Revelation 12:7.
[86] Daniel 10:21.
[87] Revelation 17:14.
[88] Jude 1:9.
[89] Matthew 4:10.
[90] Matthew 4:11.
[91] 1 Thessalonians 4:16.
[92] John 1:14; John 1:18; John 3:18 & 1 John 4:9.
[93] The word begotten is a translation of the Greek word 'monogenes.' 'Mono' means one and 'genes' means kind. So, Jesus is one of a kind.
[94] Psalm 2:7.

[95] The Greek word here is 'gennao.' This word is the equivalent of the Hebrew word 'yalad.' Both words convey the idea of 'bringing forth.' Psalm 2:7 indicates Jesus was 'brought forth' on a particular day. Given that this verse is cited in three New Testament passages which speak of the Resurrection, this verse is a prophecy of Jesus being 'brought forth' from the grave.
[96] Acts 13:32-33; Hebrews 1:5 & Hebrews 5:5.
[97] Romans 1:4.
[98] Isaiah 43:11.
[99] Titus 2:13.
[100] See Genesis 1:2; Matthew 3:16; Acts 5:3-4; Romans 8:9; Romans 8:14; 1 Corinthians 2:10-14; 1 Corinthians 3:16 and 1 Corinthians 12:3.
[101] Acts 8:29.
[102] Acts 13:2.
[103] See Acts 8:29; Acts 11:12 and Acts 13:2-4.
[104] Ephesians 4:30.
[105] Hebrews 10:29.
[106] Hebrews 9:14 and John 14:16.
[107] Romans 15:18-19.
[108] 1 Corinthians 2:10-11 and John 14:26.
[109] Genesis 1:2.
[110] Acts 5:3.
[111] Acts 5:4.
[112] Currently, to be a Seventh-day Adventist, you must accept the "28 Fundamental Beliefs" of the Seventh-day Adventist Church. One of these beliefs, called "The Gift of Prophecy," states the following: "One of the gifts of the Holy Spirit is prophecy. This gift is an identifying mark of the remnant church and was manifested in the ministry of Ellen. G. White. As the Lord's messenger, her writings are a continuing and authoritative source of truth which provide for the church comfort, guidance, instruction, and correction." Since she is thought to be "the Lord's messenger" and her writings are considered a "continuing and authoritative source of truth," Seventh-day Adventists have to believe everything Ellen G. White said was inspired of God. The "28 Fundamental Beliefs" can be found at the official Seventh-day Adventist website.
[113] White, E., *Patriarchs and Prophets*, 1958, p. 761; *Review & Herald.*
[114] Matthew 1:22-23.
[115] Quoted in *Seventh-day Adventist Bible Commentary*, vol. 5, p. 1129.

The Call

[1] This popular expression is taken from Ecclesiastes 1:9. The foundation of this section is built upon the Book of Ecclesiastes.
[2] See 2 Peter 3:3-7.
[3] John 10:9.
[4] John 3:3.
[5] John 3:7.
[6] John 1:12-13.
[7] Titus 2:11. See also Ephesians 2:8-9.

[8] 1 Corinthians 2:14.
[9] 2 Corinthians 4:4.
[10] John 3:19.
[11] 1 Timothy 2:4 and 2 Peter 3:9. See also Ezekiel 18:23.
[12] John 6:44. See also John 6:65.
[13] See John 5:31-47 for a few of the ways in which the Father testifies to Jesus.
[14] John 6:37.
[15] Ephesians 1:13.
[16] Mark 12:29-31.
[17] Matthew 12:30.
[18] 2 Peter 3:9.
[19] 1 John 2:18.
[20] Daniel 11:36 & Revelation 13:5.
[21] Revelation 7:9-14 & Revelation 13:7.
[22] Zechariah 13:8-9; Matthew 24:15-22 and Revelation 12:13-17.
[23] Daniel 8:24.
[24] Revelation 13:2.
[25] 2 Thessalonians 2:9.
[26] Matthew 24:24.
[27] See Ephesians 1:4-13.
[28] Revelation 13:16.
[29] Revelation 13:17.
[30] Matthew 24:6.
[31] Genesis 12:2-3.
[32] Genesis 26:1-5.
[33] Genesis 35:10-12.
[34] See Deuteronomy 28:64 and Leviticus 26:33.
[35] See Deuteronomy 28:65-66 and Leviticus 26:36.
[36] See Isaiah 66:22, Jeremiah 30:11 and Jeremiah 31:35-37.
[37] See Isaiah 11:10-12 and Ezekiel 36:22-28.
[38] Isaiah 66:8.
[39] John 15:18.
[40] John 15:20.
[41] See John 3:19-20.
[42] Psalm 5:5.
[43] According to *Vine's Complete Expository Dictionary of Old and New Testament Words*, the Hebrew word sane' [שָׂנֵא] (pronounced saw-nay) means "hate," as we would use it, and "set against." See Vine, W. E., Unger, Merrill F., White Jr., William. "To Hate." *Vine's Complete Expository Dictionary of Old and New Testament Words*. Nashville: Thomas Nelson, 1996.
[44] 1 John 4:8; 16.
[45] Romans 5:8.
[46] 1 Timothy 2:4.
[47] Genesis 1:26.
[48] John 3:36.
[49] Psalm 7:11.
[50] See Matthew 24:37-39.
[51] Mark 8:36.

[52] Romans 14:12.
[53] Romans 6:23.
[54] Mark 9:48.
[55] Jude 1:13.
[56] Matthew 24:51. See also Matthew 8:12; Matthew 25:30 and Luke 13:28.
[57] Revelation 14:11.
[58] Matthew 11:28.
[59] Matthew 7:13.
[60] Matthew 7:14.
[61] Matthew 10:28.
[62] John 14:6.
[63] John 18:37.
[64] Genesis 3:5.
[65] John 8:32.
[66] See 2 Corinthians 5:17; Galatians 5:22-25 and James 2:14-26.
[67] Mark 1:15. See also 1 Corinthians 15:1-4.
[68] Matthew 7:21.
[69] John 6:40.
[70] See John 3:5-8, Romans 8:9, 1 Corinthians 3:16 and 1 Corinthians 6:19.
[71] Galatians 5:22-23.
[72] John 14:26.
[73] 2 Corinthians 5:21.
[74] John 3:16.